Dining by Design

Olga Tuchscher Krasnoff

with photography by
Roberto Zeballos & Larry Stanley

ANNOTATION PRESS

A DIVISION OF WinePress PUBLISHING GROUP

Annotation Press (a division of WinePress Publishing, PO Box 428, Enumclaw, WA 98022) functions only as book publisher. As such, the ultimate design, content, editorial accuracy, and views expressed or implied in this work are those of the author.

ISBN 13: 978-1-59977-009-3
ISBN 10: 1-59977-009-1
Library of Congress Catalog Card Number: 2007922539

Printed in China.
APC-FT4720.

To my father,
Albert Benjamin Conard,
the most elegant gentleman
I have ever known and
the perfect host.

—OTK

Contents

Introduction

Dining by Design has been my mantra for two decades, and for the past ten years I have had the pleasure of teaching women of all ages how to turn an ordinary table into an extraordinary work of art.

During my tenure as senior interior designer at Macy's Home Store, tabletop specialist at Bloomingdale's, event planner for Tiffany & Co. (over fifty events), and president of Tabletop Landscapes, I have had opportunity to meet thousands of women who always express a desire to entertain with style and panache and to do it with the confidence of the professionals. That experience and interaction led to my Dining by Design seminars, at which I've taught countless women to entertain at a moment's notice with a minimum of stress, and eventually to my dream of doing this book.

Dining by Design is intended to spark your imagination when you entertain and light your passion to be the hostess you have always dreamed you could be. I know that you will fall in love, as I have, with the joy of dressing a table and entertaining, and that you will be inspired to reflect on your personal style at your next dinner party. Teaching you to say something whimsical, bold, elegant, classic, or beautiful without uttering a word, on your next tabletop and at your next dinner party, is my goal.

Take my passion to create beautiful tables and make it yours!

Sit your guests down to a beautiful table
and get up from your meal to a standing ovation.
—Olga Tuchscher Krasnoff

Inviting Invitations

*A*n affair to remember starts with the invitation you send and speaks volumes about you as well as your event. The invitation is the peak through the window to a party that you want your guests to begin to relish. The invitation you design or select and send is the start of a successful party, setting the mood and stirring an air of excitement and anticipation in the recipient.

Consider the invitation a gift to your guests, the first of many gifts they will receive as the party progresses. Select it as carefully as you would a present for a special friend. After all, guests that you are inviting are people you care about as friends, love as family, or want to impress as business associates.

Whether you're hosting a romantic dinner for two, providing a business dinner for twenty, or throwing a holiday buffet for fifty, it all starts with a trip to your favorite stationery store. If you don't have a favorite stationery store, it's time to find one as soon as possible, because there is no party without an invitation.

Call the friend who sent you that adorable invitation you saved for months and couldn't bear to throw away and ask where she bought it. Get the phone number and call the owner or manager for an appointment. The management will be thrilled to have a prospective client who cares enough to want the very best they have to offer, and it's important for you to start building a relationship with entertaining experts. Listen to them, learn from them, and take plenty of notes to put in your entertainment folder.

Ask to see the custom designs the store has produced and also take a good look at what reflects your style that is available off the shelf and in catalogs. When looking through catalogs, make a note of designs that suit your style so you won't have to guess which book they were in when you are ready to order.

Creative invitations off the shelf are very important because your time frame or your budget may not allow for custom-designed invitations. Does the store have a good variety—ethnic to elegant, hip or homey, fun and funky? Who knows what kind of party you might want to have! Finding an invitation that inspires a party theme you hadn't thought of yet is worth the time you take to peruse the invitation section of your favorite store. *What fun!* I can't tell you how many times the invitation I found inspired the affair.

If you find an invitation you love and can't live without, buy it even if you aren't giving a party for several months. You usually know how many people you like to entertain, whether a formal sit down for twelve, a patio party for twenty, or cocktails for fifty.

The services the stationery store offers, such as calligraphy, addressing and mailing, and delivery, are as important as the merchandise they carry. Write down the individual prices for their services so that there are no surprises when you want to give your next party and are figuring out your budget.

Remember, you want to be a stressless hostess, and having a store that can provide you all the reliability and services under one roof is worth its weight in gold. Saving your time and energy will be worth every penny you spend on the services rendered by the stationery store.

Once you have researched and found the perfect store to buy your invitations, you are well on your way to becoming the hostess all your friends look to as the guru of entertaining.

Entertaining Thoughts

Entertaining with style and panache is the gift we give to the family and friends we invite to share our hearth and home. The gift of style and our attention to detail when we entertain give us great satisfaction and bring untold joy to the people we host in our home.

Successful entertaining requires careful planning, organization, and a big dose of imagination! Don't worry if you don't feel you are creative. With this book as your guide, you will achieve a marvelous look on your table with a minimum of trouble. The secret is to design and create your tablescape well in advance of your event, set it, and forget it.

Style on your table is more about mood and feeling than it is about money. It's not what you have, it's what you do with what you have. My philosophy of tablescaping and entertaining is simple: Create an atmosphere on your dining table that reflects the mood and style of the event, using personal collections and things you treasure in a creative and interesting way to make your centerpiece and your party the event you dreamed of.

Tablescaping is an art that can be learned! You don't have to be an interior designer or an artist. You need to follow a few rules, break a few rules, and look at your dining room as your theater and your table as your stage. When you think about it in this way, you can become the award-winning producer and director of your next event. Let your imagination take you and your guests to an English garden, an exotic island, the French Riviera, or the African plains of the Serengeti via your tabletop landscape. Creating a story in the middle of your table is the goal, and you will be surprised at the comments and conversation it will create at your dinner table.

Our home is our haven. It's where we feel safe and comfortable and where we express ourselves. It's where we show our love to our family and friends. What better way to say welcome than by inviting your favorite people to share your hearth, home, and dinner table. It's the ultimate gift!

Entertaining and tablescaping is my passion—make it yours!

Creative invitations are crucial to the success of your event.

The Wording of your invitation entice your guests to R.S.V.P. ~ A.S.A.P.

Olga K.

Stressless Entertaining

The key to a stress-free event is being smart by exploring and using your talents, practicing what you learn in this book, and being *organized!*

First, let me assure you that you don't have to slaughter the beef, grow your own vegetables, weave your tablecloth, throw your own pots, make the dining room table, and cook the meal from scratch! Can you think of anyone in your circle of friends who does that? I can't, and I sure don't know Martha Stewart, do you?

Start by taking an inventory of all of your china, stemware, silver, flatware, linens, place-card holders, and napkin rings. This is crucial to being a successful hostess. Make two lists, one of your casualware and another of your formal settings. Perhaps you need napkin rings, chargers, or place-card holders. Once you know what you need, it's time to go shopping and complete your entertaining inventory.

Having everything to dress your table in your china cabinet is the key to being a stress-free hostess. No last-minute panic when you realize you don't have the right place mats! You should be able to set a fabulous table at a moment's notice.

Next, it's a good idea to take inventory of yourself. What do you do best? Is making flower arrangements your forte, or do you make an award-winning apple pie? Whatever it is, capitalize on your talent and show that talent off. My philosophy is to do what you do best when it comes to entertaining and use other people's talents to help you be the perfect hostess.

In other words, what you don't do the best, hire the best! No one said you have to do everything when you entertain. If you're a fabulous cook, by all means pick one of the wonderful menus and recipes in this book and cook away. If you feel more comfortable hiring a caterer, do it without feeling guilty, dress a beautiful table, and bake your award-winning dessert.

If you hire your favorite caterer, you have it made, but if you are doing the cooking, please don't be in the kitchen the entire night or you will fail as a hostess. Nothing is more irritating to guests than having their hostess in the kitchen the entire night, because they feel they should be there helping you! And don't you want to enjoy visiting with your guests? So if you decide to do the cooking, be smart selecting your menu and recipes and make as many dishes ahead as you can. If you need help to get everything done, recruit a friend or hire someone to help you before, during, and after the party.

Remember, stress-free entertaining means being organized and getting the help you need when you need it!

What I do want you to do is dress your table with style, creativity, and panache, whether it be a formal affair or funky and fun. No excuses. Pick a table you love in this book and be a copycat. Do it ahead of time. On the day of your party, I want you to take a nap so you will enjoy your affair and your company.

When the doorbell rings and you greet your guests, I want you to look gorgeous, rested, and ready to party. You decided to have this event, and you decided the theme, gathered your guest list, sent out the invitations, planned the menu, did your shopping, designed a spectacular tabletop landscape, dressed your table—and you have cooked as much as you could ahead of time or hired a caterer. Now, ring the dinner bell, escort your guests to the dining room, and get your well-deserved standing ovation!

At the Center of Attention

People are collectors and love to accumulate what they consider interesting, beautiful, or perhaps what brings back childhood memories—everything from miniature boxes to duck decoys, antique dolls, quilts, and exotic ceramic animals. Whatever treasures you collect express something about you, who you are, and what you love. Start now to take inventory of your collections, because I want you to consider using what you collect, treasure, and love for your next centerpiece.

The centerpiece, in my point of view, is not just to create esthetic beauty but to stimulate conversation by elevating those special treasures to individual works of art on your dinner table. I collect miniature porcelain boxes, perfume bottles, Lalique, antique teacups, as well as Lladro figurines, chickens, and roosters. My husband has a fabulous collection of apples. All have been the focus of a centerpiece at my breakfast, luncheon, or dinner table. My girlfriend collects chrome and glass contemporary sculptures and uses those beautiful pieces as part of her centerpieces. Both express our individual personalities. Both are perfect. There is no right or wrong.

Your collections, whatever they may be, will become works of art on your table and will become the focal point of your next centerpiece. Start by taking a good look around your home. What do you collect and treasure? Gather these items on your table.

Then place boxes (acrylic or cardboard, small or large gift boxes or shoe boxes) in the center of your table, and cover the boxes with a smaller tablecloth or piece of fabric that reflects the style of your dinner party. That fabric might be damask for a very formal affair or a checked gingham for a country affair. These draped boxes become pedestals that elevate your collection into a miniature work of art as you lovingly place your treasures on top of them.

Now place some vines, flowers, straw, or moss (whatever is appropriate) in and around your collection. *Voila!* You have an unusual, interesting and smashing centerpiece. At a moment's notice, all you had to do is go to your curio cabinet, pull out the things you love, put them in the middle of your table, and you are already on your way to becoming a tablescaper extraordinaire!

What you create when you tablescape is not only an unusual and stunning centerpiece but conversation. Sit back and enjoy sharing how you started the collection, where you purchased the items, and how long you have been a collector. Don't forget to ask your guests what they collect.

We know that Paris, New York, and Hollywood once defined style for the rest of the world, and now you are going to define style for your family, friends, business associates, and your social set!

The Jewels of the Table

A table is transformed from ordinary to extraordinary by the attention to detail at every place setting—the jewels of the table. These items should be at every sit-down event you have, whether it's breakfast, lunch, or dinner:

- the charger
- the menu card
- the napkin ring
- the place-card holder
- the place card
- the favor

The *charger* frames your china and can change the whole complexion of the event depending on its color, elegance, or whimsy. I like it to remain on the table during all of the courses, including dessert.

The *menu card* can be tucked into a napkin, placed on the dinner plate at every place setting, or positioned in a frame somewhere on the table or the buffet. It is a detail your guests will immediately notice and that shows your attention to all aspects of the event.

The *napkin ring* dresses up an ordinary napkin or enhances a beautiful one. One of the stars of the table, the selections are incredible: sterling silver, ceramic, enamel, acrylic, gold, and colored glass; roosters, butterflies, fans, teapots, fish, and flowers are just a sampling of napkin rings you can purchase.

When you see one you like, buy at least twelve; I promise you won't regret it!

The *place-card holder* may be simple as a store-bought paper place card, a frame with your guest's name or picture, a porcelain holder that you can write on and use again and again, or something more creative, such as luggage tags for a travel reunion party. There are hundreds of designs to choose from.

The *place card* not only dresses the table but helps you control the seating. Where to sit the boss and his wife can be very important, and you want to make sure Uncle Harry and Aunt Grace don't cause a family disruption at your table with their political ranting!

The *favor* is that extra little touch that shows each guest you truly care: a miniature box of candy, a silver wine stopper, a lovely ceramic box with the date and occasion of the party, a small box of stationery, or a small frame that doubles as a place-card holder—put a picture of your guest in the frame. A wonderful memory of the event!

"The Jewels of the table are what turn an ordinary table into an extraordinary work of art!"

Olga K.

The Brunch Bunch

A beautifully dressed table can turn a meal into a feast, a house into a home, and a stranger into a friend.

Living "The Big Easy"

*A*dmiral Leon "Bud" Edney, USN (retired), and his wife, Margon, have entertained dignitaries around the world with formal elegance and style, but have chosen to live the good life in their French-inspired Coronado, California, home. Entertaining their family and friends in the warmth and charm of their country French kitchen on a Sunday morning is one of their greatest pleasures. I invite you to join us there now for brunch surrounded by sunflowers, a crowing rooster, a friendly French chicken, and the best New Orleans cuisine we could muster.

Please Come For
Fine Food and Family Fun
at The Edny's
Sunday June 26th
Brunch 11 O'CLOCK
Memories & Music 1 O'CLOCK
Regrets Only 444-5687

The Tabletop Landscape

A red and yellow checked tablecloth compliments the red rooster embroidered fabric on the bar stools.

Golden yellow, green, and tomato-red chargers with matching potteryware, all adorned with French roosters, lie on twig placements. For a change of pace, leaf-shaped plates with poppy-covered bowls compliment the setting. Tomato-red fringed napkins are held with a black iron napkin ring. Stemware in golden-yellow hues stand among fresh-cut sunflowers, with flatware in yellow gingham and chevron stripes adding to the ambience.

Yellow black-eyed daisies tied with toile ribbon grace the back of every bar stool as an invitation to sit and be comfortable.

A happy iron chicken and a confident rooster meander through the straw and sunflower field, and a wreath of herbs and dried flowers in matching colors hangs from the copper hood as the perfect background to frame and finish the table.

Quick Tips

- Sunflowers stay fresh by putting them in individual water tubes that can be purchased at your local florist or floral supply store.
- Scatter hay on the tablecloth and scatter the sunflowers casually down the center of the table.
- Mixing and matching your dinnerware is the element of surprise that defines the country French style.

- Layering is an interesting way to add dimension to your table. On this table, we used a tablecloth, layered it with straw, used twigs as placemats, and then added the sunflowers, the china, crystal flatware, and napkins.
- Blue and yellow (the colors in Claude Monet's kitchen in Giverny) are colors that exude the country French style.

COMMANDER'S PALACE

1403 Washington Avenue
New Orleans, Louisiana

Tory McPhail
Executive Chef

Since 1880 Commander's Palace has been a New Orleans landmark known for the award winning quality of its food and its beautiful interior—as timeless and treasured as its gardens.

As executive chef at the famed restaurant, 30-year-old Tory McPhail has big clogs to fill, following in the steps of household names like Paul Prudhomme, Emeril Lagasse and Jamie Shannon. There is no doubt the Brennans have an eye for spotting the country's top culinary talents, and with McPhail—a James Beard Rising Star Chef Nominee during his first year at the helm—they have done it again. He is proud to take his place as the latest of great chefs to assume leadership of the Commander's kitchen as he guides the restaurant in its culinary mission: The evolution of haute Creole cuisine.

Menu

❧ *Shrimp Remoulade*

❧ *Garden District Eggs
with Tasso Hollandaise*

❧ *Pain Perdu*

Shrimp Remoulade
8 servings

When dipping sauce is well chilled, serve with peeled, boiled shrimp (approximately 5–7 shrimp per person).

REMOULADE SAUCE

Yield: 2½ cups

3	garlic cloves, peeled
1½	celery ribs, chopped
¼	cup egg substitute
2	tablespoons ketchup
2	tablespoons prepared horseradish
2	tablespoons Creole mustard
2	tablespoons yellow mustard
2	tablespoons mild paprika
1/2	tablespoon Worcestershire sauce
1½	tablespoons hot sauce (or to taste)
1/2	teaspoon ground red pepper
3/4	cup vegetable oil
3	green onions, sliced

Kosher salt and black pepper to taste

Process first 12 ingredients in a blender or food processor until smooth. With blender running, add oil in a slow, steady stream until mixture is thickened. Stir in green onions, salt, and black pepper; cover and chill until ready to serve.

Chef's Notes
- You can make the sauce up to several days ahead.

Garden District Eggs
with Tasso Hollandaise

8 servings

You don't need a platoon of chefs to prepare this recipe, so don't be intimidated. Use the timeline that follows the recipes to produce a dish that will dazzle your guests.

16 POACHED EGGS

2 (6-ounce) packages fresh spinach

1 tablespoon water

Mushroom Cakes *(see recipe that follows)*

Tasso Hollandaise *(see recipe that follows)*

2 pounds steamed asparagus (optional)

Garnishes: finely chopped red bell pepper,
    chopped fresh parsley

Cook spinach and 1 tablespoon water in a large nonstick skillet over medium heat 5 minutes or until wilted, stirring once; drain well. Place ¼ cup spinach on each of 8 serving plates; top with two mushroom cakes. Top with 2 poached eggs and hollandaise. Serve with asparagus, if desired. Garnish, if desired.

MUSHROOM CAKES

1 cup butter (2 sticks)

1 medium onion, finely chopped

1 medium green bell pepper, finely chopped

1 medium red bell pepper, finely chopped

7 garlic cloves, minced

½ pound assorted wild mushrooms, sliced

1 pound fresh mushrooms, sliced

1 (16-ounce) French bread loaf, cut into
    1-inch cubes

4 large eggs, lightly beaten

1 cup fine dry breadcrumbs

1 (32-ounce) container chicken broth

1/3 cup each chopped fresh basil, thyme,
    and oregano

2 bunches green onions, chopped

1 teaspoon salt

1 teaspoon pepper

Vegetable cooking spray

Melt butter in a Dutch oven over medium heat; add onion, peppers, and garlic; sauté 10 minutes or until tender.

Add mushrooms and cook 30 minutes or until liquid evaporates. Stir in bread cubes, lightly beaten eggs, and breadcrumbs. Gradually stir in chicken broth until the mixture resembles stuffing. Stir in herbs, green onions, salt, and pepper. Cover and chill 8 hours.

Shape mixture into 16 cakes, using about ¾ cup mixture for each. Coat a nonstick griddle or large nonstick skillet with cooking spray. Cook cakes in batches over medium-high heat, 4 minutes on each side or until golden. Place cakes on a wire rack in a jellyroll pan and keep warm in a 200° oven.

TASSO HOLLANDAISE

Yield: 3 cups

8 egg yolks

¼ cup fresh lemon juice

2 tablespoons white wine

2 cups (1 pound) butter, melted

½ teaspoon salt

1/8 teaspoon ground red pepper

½ cup finely chopped tasso ham (about 6
    ounces)*

    * ½ cup diced, cooked andouille sausage
    may be substituted.

Whisk yolks in top of a double boiler; gradually whisk in lemon juice and wine. Place over hot water (do not boil). Add butter, 1/3 cup at a time, whisking until smooth; whisk in salt and red pepper. Cook, whisking constantly, 10 minutes or until thickened and a thermometer registers 160°. Stir in tasso ham. Serve immediately.

Express method: Prepare 2 (9-ounce) packages hollandaise sauce mix according to package directions; stir in tasso ham.

Timeline for Garden District Eggs with Tasso Hollandaise

You can prepare this dish in four make-ahead components. For a refresher course on poaching eggs, see the step-by-step photos at southernliving.com/features. If you're reluctant to poach the eggs, you can scramble or fry them instead.

Two days ahead:
- Chop the vegetables and mushrooms and place in zip-top plastic bags; chill.
- Cube the bread and store in a zip-top plastic bag.

One day ahead:
- Make mushroom cakes mixture; chill.

Day of brunch:
- Cook mushroom cakes up to 1 hour ahead; cover loosely and keep warm in a 200° oven.
- Make the Tasso Hollandaise; keep warm in a thermal container or very clean insulated coffee carafe.
- Steam the asparagus, if serving.
- Cook the spinach. Cover and keep warm.
- Poach the eggs.
- Assemble the egg dish; serve asparagus on the side.

The good company of dear friends at your table is a gift to treasure.

Pain Perdu
8–12 servings

In the French language, French toast is a pain perdu, or "lost bread," because it's made from stale bread.

- 2 (16-ounce) French bread loaves
- 8 large eggs
- 4 cups whipping cream
- 1 cup sugar
- ½–1 tablespoon ground cinnamon
- 1½ teaspoons ground nutmeg
- 4 teaspoons vanilla extract
- 1½ cups champagne
- 2 cups cane syrup
- 4 cups raspberries and blueberries
- 4 tablespoons cream cheese (optional)

Garnish: powdered sugar

Cut bread into 24 diagonal slices, ¾ inches thick. Whisk together eggs and next 5 ingredients until well blended.

Place bread slices in a 13 x 9 inch baking dish; pour egg mixture evenly over slices. Let stand 30 minutes or until liquid is absorbed.

Remove bread slices from egg mixture, letting excess drip off. Cook bread slices in batches in a lightly greased nonstick skillet or griddle over medium-high heat, 2 minutes on each side or until golden. Place bread slices on baking sheets; keep warm in a 200° oven.

Cook champagne in a large saucepan over high heat until reduced by half. Gradually stir in syrup; cook over low heat until blended and warm.

Arrange bread slices on serving plates; top with raspberries, blueberries and, if desired, cream cheese. Drizzle evenly with syrup mixture. Garnish, if desired.

Willow Tree Garden Brunch

Summer sunshine and welcome shade under my willow tree always transport me to a time when, as a child, I made a lazy trip on a paddle wheeler up the Mississippi River with my grandmother. We stopped in New Orleans, where family and friends waited with anticipation and then entertained us in their backyard with family stories of days gone by and served us mouthwatering southern cooking.

The corner of my yard where my majestic willow tree beckons and invites nostalgia is the perfect location for sharing those memories and re-creating those moments with my best friends, who appreciate and enjoy the ambience of that time long ago when ladies fanned themselves in the warmth of the sun, enjoyed true friendship, and shared tasty food and delicious gossip.

Under my willow tree surrounded by fragrant flowers is a delightful spot to share precious time with my dearest friends, the "ladies" I love.

The Tabletop Landscape

Battenberg lace and a crisp floral chintz tablecloth romance the garden and set the stage for watering cans sitting on moss, filled with fresh flowers. Mini terra-cotta pots are scattered around the watering cans, while sparkling white lacelike chargers, floral petal stemware, elegant silverware, and a wreath of fresh flowers at every place setting adds to the garden ambience.

Miniature watering cans filled with dainty flowers serve as napkin rings and place-card holders to continue the theme. Guests take home Battenberg lace umbrellas as a keepsake of a day in my garden.

Quick Tips

- Bring your garden to your tabletop by setting flower-filled watering cans on your table and then building up moss in and around the cans, as if they were growing out of the moss.
- Fill mini terra-cotta pots with small clumps of flowers like alyssum or lantana and scatter the pots casually on the moss around the watering cans.
- A miniature watering can (available in craft stores) filled with mini flowers can hold the place card. The handle becomes the napkin ring, and guests can take home the watering can as their favor.
- Surround your charger with a ring of fresh flowers to enhance the garden tablescape theme.

COMMANDER'S PALACE

1403 Washington Avenue
New Orleans, Louisiana

Tory McPhail
Executive Chef

When I eat Bread Pudding Soufflé, I always think of the Commander's saying, "If it ain't broke, fix it anyway." Our bread pudding was already near perfection, but we combined Creole bread pudding with the light texture of meringue and ended up with the restaurant's signature dessert, the single most sought-after dish in our family's restaurant history. The whiskey sauce itself is divine, but particularly so when generously poured over the piping hot soufflé. Take it from me, this is no light dessert! Make the bread pudding and the sauce in advance, the meringue just before assembling and baking.

—Ti Adelaide Martin, restaurant co-owner

Menu

❧ *Bloody Mary*

❧ *Catfish Pecan with Lemon Thyme Pecan Butter*

❧ *Eggs Sardou*

❧ *Bread Pudding Soufflé with Whisky Sauce*

Bloody Mary

1 serving

1½ ounces vodka

1 teaspoon prepared horseradish

1 teaspoon or 2 splashes Worcestershire sauce

2 dashes hot sauce

½ cup vegetable juice or tomato juice

Garnishes: Creole seasoning, either seafood or meat; 1 each pickled pepper and pickled okra, skewered with sugarcane or toothpick

Fill an old-fashioned glass two-thirds full with ice cubes and add vodka, horseradish, Worcestershire, hot sauce, and vegetable juice. Cover with a shaker and shake; then let rest in shaker.

Wet rim of glass and place in Creole seasoning, coating the entire rim of glass. Pour drink back into glass and garnish with okra and pepper.

Chef's Notes

- I like to use V8® juice if I don't have access to fresh-squeezed vegetables.
- An old-fashioned glass is another name for a rocks glass. You can use any 12-ounce cocktail glass.
- If you like extra seasoning, as I do, season the top of the drink with fresh cracked pepper and kosher salt.

© Lori Sparkia. Shutterstock.

Catfish Pecan with Lemon Thyme Pecan Butter

6 servings

3 cups pecans, chopped

1½ cups flour

2 teaspoons or more Creole seafood seasoning or favorite seasoning

1 medium egg

1 cup milk

6 catfish filets (6–8 ounces each)*

1½ sticks butter (6 ounces)

3 lemons, cut in half

1 tablespoon Worcestershire sauce

Salt and pepper to taste

Garnish: ¼ ounce fresh thyme or 6 large sprigs

> ** Flounder, trout, bass, or any thin, smaller non-oily fish may be substituted.*

Add ½ cup pecans and the flour to a food processor and season with Creole seasoning. Process until fine. Remove and place in a large bowl.

In a separate bowl, whisk egg and add milk. Add Creole seasoning. Check fish to be sure it is free of any bones or scales. Place into egg wash. Repeat with all filets.

Remove one filet; drain excess egg wash back into bowl. Place filet into pecan flour mixture and coat both sides. Shake off any excess mixture and place filet on a dry cookie sheet. Repeat with remaining filets.

Place a large sauté pan over high heat and add ¼ stick of butter. Heat for about 2 minutes or until butter is completely melted and starts to bubble. Place 3 fish filets in pan, skin side up, and cook 30 seconds; reduce heat to medium.

Cook until coating is brown and crisp, about 1 minute, 45 seconds or 2 minutes. Turn fish over and cook 2–2½ minutes, or until done. Fish should be firm to the touch and brown in color.

Remove fish and place on a rack. Wipe pan clean with paper towel. Add ¼ stick butter and repeat with the three filets.

When all fish is cooked, wipe pan clean and return heat to high. Add remaining 1 stick butter and melt about 2 minutes, or until just turning brown. Add remaining 1½ cups pecans and sauté 2–3 minutes or until toasted, stirring occasionally. Add lemons, squeezing a little juice from each and placing face down. Add Worcestershire and fresh thyme. Season with salt and pepper and cook an additional 30 seconds, or until thyme starts to wilt and becomes very aromatic.

Serve fish with a lemon piece and spoon pecan butter over fish. Garnish with wilted thyme.

Chef's Notes

- This dish requires a little more butter when sautéing. You don't want to burn the nuts on the crust.
- When making the browned butter with pecans, don't brown butter too much or it will become bitter.
- Sauté time will depend on thickness of the fish. You might want to finish fish in oven if it is too thick, so you don't burn the crust.

© Winthrop Brookhouse. Shutterstock.

Eggs Sardou

8 servings

  2 pounds fresh spinach

  ½ stick or 4 tablespoons butter

  ¼ cup flour

  1 cup heavy cream

  1 teaspoon nutmeg

  Salt and pepper to taste

  16 medium or large artichokes

  2 lemons

  ¼ cup whole black peppercorns

  16 poached eggs

  2 cups hollandaise

Clean spinach by discarding any large stems and brown leaves. Wash in cold water three times and tear spinach into 3-inch pieces. Let drain and set aside.

In a large pot over medium heat, melt butter (about 2 minutes). Slowly add flour, constantly stirring with a wooden spoon, and cook for about 2 minutes or until roux is pale and smells lightly nutty and has the consistency of wet sand.

Stir in cream, nutmeg, and salt and pepper. Simmer for about 2 minutes, stirring constantly until smooth. Add half the spinach and stir. Cook for about 3 minutes. Add remaining spinach, stir and cook until tender (about 4–6 minutes). Adjust seasoning and consistency by adding more cream or cooking longer to reduce liquid.

Cut stems off artichokes. In an even manner, place artichokes upside down tightly in a large pot, stacking at least two layers high.

Using a pitcher, measure one quart water. Slice lemons and add juice and lemons to water. Add peppercorns and season with salt. Stir and pour over artichokes. Place pot over high heat and cover. Bring to a boil and steam for 30–40 minutes or until done. If artichoke hearts are tender when pricked with a knife, or if large leaves pull off with little resistance, artichokes are ready.

When artichokes are done, remove from water and run cold water over them to stop the cooking process, then peel. Scrape out the artichoke with a spoon.

To serve, place about ½ cup of creamed spinach on center of a hot plate. Place 2 hot artichoke bottoms in center of creamed spinach and place a poached egg in the center of each artichoke heart. Spoon about an ounce (2 tablespoons) of hollandaise over each egg.

Chef's Notes

- If you don't want to do all your cooking in the morning, you can cook your creamed spinach and artichokes in advance. Store cooked artichoke bottoms in water.
- Be sure you cut the artichoke bottoms evenly, so eggs will not roll off.
- Keep plates, spinach, and artichokes very hot, so your dish makes it to the table hot after you add the eggs and hollandaise.
- Be careful not to overcook artichokes.
- Drain artichokes and eggs; use a towel to pat dry before adding sauce.

© Andi Berger. Shutterstock.

Bread Pudding Soufflé with Whiskey Sauce

6 servings

¾ cup sugar

1 teaspoon ground cinnamon

Pinch of nutmeg

3 medium eggs

1 cup heavy cream

1 teaspoon vanilla extract

5 cups New Orleans French bread, 1 inch cubes (see note)

1/3 cup raisins

Meringue *(see recipe that follows)*

Whiskey Sauce *(see recipe that follows)*

Preheat oven to 350° and grease an 8-inch-square baking pan. Combine sugar, cinnamon, and nutmeg in a large bowl. Beat in the eggs until smooth; then work in the heavy cream. Add the vanilla and bread cubes. Allow bread to soak up custard.

Place the raisins in the greased pan. Top with the egg mixture, which prevents the raisins from burning. Bake for approximately 25–30 minutes or until the pudding has a golden brown color and is firm to the touch. If a toothpick inserted in the pudding comes out clean, pudding is done. The texture of pudding should be moist, not runny or dry. Cool to room temperature.

In a large bowl, break half the bread pudding into pieces, using your hands or a spoon. Gently fold in one-fourth of the meringue, being careful not to lose the air in the whites. Add a portion of this base to each of the ramekins.

Place the remaining bread pudding in the bowl, break into pieces, and carefully fold in the rest of the meringue. Top off the soufflés with this lighter mixture, to about 1½ inches above the top of the ramekins. Smooth and shape with spoon into a dome over the ramekin rim.

Bake immediately for approximately 20 minutes or until golden brown. Serve immediately. Using a spoon, poke a hole in the top of each soufflé, at the table, and pour the room-temperature whiskey sauce inside the soufflé.

MERINGUE

9 medium egg whites

¾ cup sugar

¼ teaspoon cream of tartar

To make the meringue, preheat oven to 350°. Butter 6 (6-ounce) ramekins.

In a large bowl or mixer, whip egg whites and cream of tartar until foamy. Add the sugar gradually, and continue whipping until whites are shiny and thick. Test with a clean spoon. If the whites stand up stiff like shaving cream when you pull out the spoon, the meringue is ready. Do not over-whip or the whites will break down and the soufflé will not work.

WHISKEY SAUCE

1 cup heavy cream

½ tablespoon cornstarch

1 tablespoon water

3 tablespoons sugar

¼ cup bourbon

Place the cream in a small saucepan over medium heat and bring to a boil. Whisk cornstarch and water together, and add to cream while whisking. Bring to a boil. Whisk and let simmer for a few seconds, taking care not to burn the mixture on the bottom. Remove from heat.

Stir in the sugar and the bourbon. Taste to make sure the sauce has a thick consistency, a sufficiently sweet taste, and a good bourbon flavor. Cool to room temperature.

Chef's Notes

- New Orleans French bread is very light and tender. If substitute bread is used that is too dense, it will soak up all the custard and the recipe won't work.
- This dish needs a good stiff meringue. Before making the meringue, be certain that the bowl and whisk are clean. The egg whites should be completely free of yolk, and they will whip better if the chill is off them.

What's on the table is important. . . . That combined with who you put in the chairs is the recipe for success.

City Slickers Country Day

City-slicker friends love an invitation to a day in the country when they get a chance to put on denim duds, cowboy hats, and Tony Lama boots and become cowpokes for a day.

Catching up with special friends at a bruncheon (a meal not as light as breakfast or as heavy as dinner) of refreshing drinks and delicious food is followed by a rodeo, hayrides, country singing, guitar picking, and even line dancing.

Our hosts Mario and Kathy Matranga graciously open their home in Alpine, California, where all city slickers can enjoy some down-home hospitality.

Y'all come, ya hear!

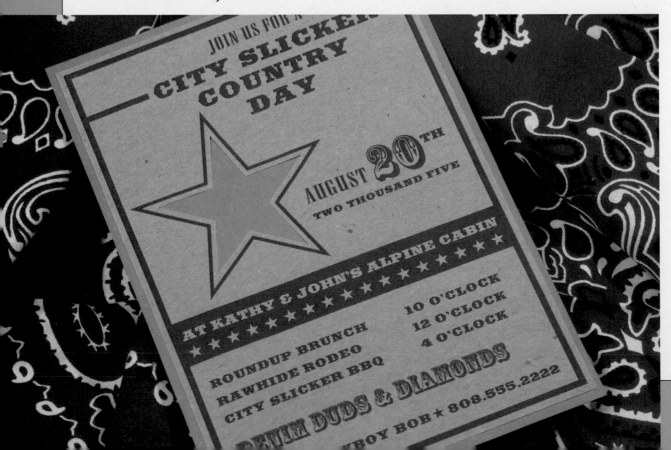

The Tabletop Landscape

An antique buckboard on bandana print fabric, brimming with sunflowers, gerbera daisies, chickens, hay, and mini cowboy boots is the center of attention at this rancher's table.

Denim placemats with pockets holding the gingham-edged napkins and colorful flatware along with enamelware chargers, dishes, and mugs complete the cowboy theme. The stemware is emblazoned with a branding-iron motif.

Mini hay bales tied with gingham ribbon are the place cards, and mini jam jars filled with homemade preserves are the favors.

Quick Tips

- Bandana prints exude a cowboy country theme as do red gingham, straw hay bales, horseshoes, and branding irons.
- The menu card can be printed on a mini checked red paper bought at a scrapbooking store, or cut an 8 x 10 inch piece from a brown paper bag and burn the edges for that rustic ranch look. Glue the menu to the checked paper. For a finished look, glue a small bunch of wheat tied with rawhide or bandana-print ribbon to one side of the menu.
- Denim fabric screams cowpokes and country casual. Make a tablecloth or placements out of denim and sew the hem with red thread. Add a pocket to the left side of the placemats to hold napkins and utensils.
- No calligraphy for name cards at a rancher's table! Write guests' names on 3 x 4 inch pieces of brown paper bag and burn the edges. Paper punch a hole in one corner, string a gingham ribbon or rawhide through the hole, and tie on a miniature hay bale or a stalk of wheat.
- Put an elegant spin on your hoe down by making it a "Denim Duds and Diamonds" party. Diamonds should start shining on the invitation and carry through all the decorations at your party, including your diamond-studded jeans!

art was recognized by industry-revered chefs.

Clay's culinary skills were acquired in a myriad of kitchens across the country. He absorbed different styles of cooking in the northeastern United States, Florida, Texas, New Mexico, and California, developing a unique cooking style all his own.

Clay has been crafting his culinary talent since 1986 and has received numerous awards and accolades. He has produced and executed award-winning restaurants and bars in key markets, including Santa Fe, New Mexico; San Diego, California; as well as South Bay, San Francisco; and he is recognized for developing concepts that reverberate throughout the restaurant, from delectable recipes and unique menus to the carefully selected interior milieu.

SANTA FE SALSA COMPANY

Traditions Marketplace
Algodones, New Mexico

Clay Bordan
Corporate Executive Chef

Corporate executive chef Clay Bordan brings finely honed expertise and a colorful flair to all his culinary creations for the American Property Management Corporation and was lured into the culinary world when his passion for food and eye for

Menu

❧ *New Mexico Green Chile Stew*

❧ *Iceburg Wedges with Toasted Piñon and Chipotle Ranch Dressing*

❧ *Mini Stuffed Sopapillas with Green Chile Sauce*

❧ *Braised Short Ribs Adobado in Hatch New Mexico Red Chile Sauce*

❧ *Taos-Style Pinto Beans*

❧ *Panfried Papitas*

❧ *Grilled Calabasitas*

❧ *Natillas*

New Mexico Green Chile Stew

6–8 servings

1 pound green chile, diced

2 tomatoes, diced

¼ onion, diced

1 tablespoon chopped garlic

2 cubes chicken bouillon

2 quarts water

3 cups peeled and diced potatoes

Salt and pepper to taste

3 tablespoons olive oil

Garnish: shredded jack cheese; tortilla chips

Place onions, tomatoes, and green chile in a saucepan and sauté until halfway cooked. Add water, garlic, bouillon, and potatoes. Simmer until potatoes are cooked through. Adjust with salt and pepper to taste. Serve in a bowl and garnish with shredded jack cheese and tortilla chips.

© Maja Schon. Shutterstock.

Iceberg Wedges with Toasted Pinon and Chipotle Ranch Dressing

6 servings

2 heads of iceberg lettuce, cleaned

2 fresh ears of corn, cooked and kernels removed

3 avocados, peeled and chopped
Chipotle Ranch Dressing (*see recipe that follows*)

Toasted Pinon (pine nuts) (*see recipe that follows*)

Garnish: chopped cilantro; Mexican cheese

Cut heads of lettuce in quarters and place in the center of a plate. In a hot sauté pan. place 1 tablespoon olive oil and the corn kernels; sauté until browned. Remove and place on a plate lined with a paper towel to remove excess grease. Drizzle each wedge of lettuce with dressing and sprinkle equal parts of diced avocado, sautéed corn, and Mexican cheese. Gently sprinkle toasted pine nuts around the wedge and chopped cilantro as garnish.

CHIPOTLE RANCH DRESSING

1 bottle of any bottled ranch dressing

1 tablespoon dried or liquid chipotle (adjust on this depending on the heat of the chipotle)

TOASTED PINON

Place pine nuts on a cookie sheet and place in 350° oven for approximately 5 minutes or until the pine nuts are browned.

Mini Stuffed Sopapillas with Green Chile Sauce

6 servings.

1 cup white flour

1 teaspoon baking powder

2 tablespoons lard

½ teaspoon salt

1/3 cup water

Vegetable oil, as needed

1 cup grilled chicken, chopped

1 cup shredded lettuce

½ cup chopped tomato

1 cup shredded cheese

Green Chile Sauce *(see recipe that follows)*

Sift together the flour, baking powder, and salt. Add lard and work in well with a pastry cutter. Add water and mix until dough is of a smooth consistency (not crumbly or sticky).

On a floured cutting board, roll out dough to 1/8 inch thickness; cut dough into 4-inch triangles.

In a deep saucepan, pour oil to 4 inches deep and heat to approximately 400°. Very carefully deep-fry sopapillas until golden brown on each side. Remove and drain on paper towels.

When cool, gently cut sopapillas open and fill with grilled chicken, lettuce, tomato, cheese. Cover with green chile sauce.

Chef's Note

• These can sometimes be tricky to make. Be careful when flipping over in the pan and show some patience and don't get discouraged. They should come out like small puffed footballs.

GREEN CHILE SAUCE

2 pounds green chiles, chopped

½ onion, diced

1 tablespoon chopped garlic

2 tomatoes, chopped

Salt and pepper, to taste

½ teaspoon ground cumin

1 quart water

1 cube chicken bouillon

Place all ingredients in a saucepan and cook for approximately 1 hour on low heat.

Braised Short Ribs Adobado in Hatch New Mexico Red Chile Sauce

6 servings

Place short ribs in a braising pan and cover with chile sauce. Simmer on low until meat becomes soft and almost falling apart.

HATCH NEW MEXICO RED CHILE SAUCE

1 pound red chile pods

2 tablespoons chopped garlic

1 tablespoon ground thyme

Salt and pepper to taste

Handful tortilla chips

Cover chile pods in water and soak for up to 1 hour, or until pods become soft. Place chile pods, garlic, salt and pepper, thyme, and tortilla chips in a blender or food processor with water reserved from the soaking process and blend well. Remove and strain through a strainer to remove skins. Transfer to a saucepan and simmer to blend flavors for approximately 30 minutes. Add water during simmering so that sauce does not become too thick. Adjust taste with salt and pepper.

Taos-Style Pinto Beans

6–8 servings

3 cups dried pinto beans

½ cup onion, diced

2 cups red chile peppers, chopped

½ cup green chile peppers, chopped

2 whole bulbs garlic, roasted

2 tablespoons chipotle sauce

Salt and pepper to taste

2 cans beer

Cover pinto beans in cold water and soak overnight to tenderize. Drain water and place beans in a saucepan with remaining ingredients; simmer on low, covered, for approximately 2–3 hours or until beans are cooked through and tender. Adding small amounts of water to compensate for reduction may be necessary. Adjust spices to individual taste throughout cooking.

Panfried Papitas

6 servings

5 large potatoes, peeled

Salt and pepper to taste

2 tablespoons olive oil

Cut potatoes in ¼-inch cubes and boil in water until fully cooked; drain and place in a nonstick sauté pan with olive oil over medium-high heat. With a spatula, give a little pressure on the potatoes to blend, which helps make a crispier crust. Cook until browned, and season with salt and pepper to taste.

Grilled Calabasitas

6 servings

3 zucchini (¼-inch cut)

3 yellow squash (¼-inch cut)

1 medium yellow onion, quartered

1 fresh ear of corn, cooked and kernels removed

1 cup chopped green chile peppers

Salt and pepper to taste

Olive oil

In an oiled sauté pan, place the zucchini, squash, onion, and corn. Cook until vegetables become almost transparent; add green chile, salt, and pepper, and continue to cook until vegetables become browned.

Natillas

6 servings

4 egg yolks

¼ cup cornstarch

4 cups condensed milk

¾ cup sugar

¼ cup vanilla extract

4 egg whites

Cinnamon, as needed

Garnish: almond ladyfingers, raspberry sauce (optional)

In a small bowl, place egg yolks, cornstarch, and 1 cup condensed milk. Stir together to make a smooth paste.

In a medium saucepan, place the remaining 3 cups of condensed milk, sugar, and vanilla. Stir constantly over medium heat until milk is scalded. Add the egg yolk mixture and continue to cook until custard thickens, stirring constantly. Remove and let cool at room temperature.

In a small bowl, beat egg whites until stiff but not dry. Fold into the custard. Place the custard in individual goblets and chill. Garnish with cinnamon, almond ladyfingers, and a dash of raspberry sauce, if desired.

"True Elegance is simplicity. Simplicity creates style!"

Olga K.

Let's Do Lunch

*Nothing is sweeter
than lunch with the ladies.*

Birdhouse Couture

*I*nterior designer Carol Raiter loves to entertain in the beautiful Cape Cod-inspired house she and her husband, Eric, designed, built, and decorated. Carol's brilliant sense of style and love of the traditional shows in every corner of her home and shines brightly when she entertains.

Always an innovator, Carol invited local artists to design and build birdhouses that could be auctioned at a charity luncheon/fashion show to benefit local garden clubs that help to beautify Coronado Island. Carol's placement of the birdhouses among her favorite trees and flowers in her magnificent garden delighted her guests, who wandered the garden choosing the birdhouses they would bid on.

Carol's gracious hospitality is always a delightful experience for every guest lucky enough to be invited to one of her parties.

The Tabletop Landscape

Birdcages brimming with pink and white roses and hydrangeas are topped by flowing celadon silk ribbons and surrounded by bird nests holding fine-feathered friends.

Carol's Italian porcelain figurine, a gift from her mother, is content sitting in her tabletop garden, adding a personal touch as it completes this centerpiece.

Galax-leaf placemats hold seeded-glass-and-gold-rimmed chargers, floral china, pink crystal stemware, and sterling silverware—the elegance that makes this garden table special.

Handblown glass flower napkin rings hold crochet-edged celadon napkins, and a hand-painted mini birdhouse serves both as the place card and favor.

Quick Tips

- The menu card, one of the jewels of the table, can be put in frame (5 x 7 is a good size) and easily tucked in and about the centerpiece
- Look for a frame that coordinates with your tabletop décor or buy a plain wood frame you can decorate to coordinate with your linens and tableware.
- The menu card can be done on your computer. Look for appropriate fonts that coordinate with your party. For a formal table, use the font French Script MT. Use black ink so people can read the menu card easily.
- A miniature birdcage gilded with gold spray paint or a miniature porcelain bird tied with a narrow ribbon in a color that compliments the tabletop décor could serve as a place card and a table favor.

~~~~~~~~~~

Menu

– *Duck Crepes*

– *Dover Sole with Lobster and Asparagus, Spaghetti Squash*

– *Pommes Gaufrette, and Citus Beurre Blanc*

– *Warm Gingerbread with Caramel Sauce, Vanilla Crème Fraiche, and Raspberries*

CHEZ LOMA FRENCH BISTRO

1132 Loma Avenue
Coronado, California

Ken Irvine

Executive Chef
President K.R.I. Inc.
Hospitality Industry Consultant

Every visitor to Coronado, California, recognizes a romantic restaurant called Chez Loma in a beautiful grey Victorian house.

Executive chef and former owner Ken Irvine, a graduate of the Culinary Institute of America in Hyde Park, New York, was on a flight to Europe the day after graduation to fine-tune his culinary skills in London and France. After great success in various award-winning restaurants in Europe, Ken's association with chef Andre Surmain and working at the Michelin-starred Relais du Mougin, just north of Cannes, inspired him to open his own restaurant on the magical island of Coronado, California, where he garnered awards such as Best French Restaurant, given by the California Restaurant Association (CRA) in 2003; Chef of the Year 2002, from the San Diego chapter of the California Restaurant Association; Best Chef, *San Diego Magazine;* as well as nominations for Restaurateur of the Year by the CRA.

Chef Irvine has participated in many events, including "Great Chefs of San Diego," and hosted the Time Warner Cable television show *Chez Chef Culinary Adventures.* He has had numerous recipes featured in local and national publications, including *Bon Appétit* magazine.

As principal of KRI, Inc., Ken provides a spectrum of services to the restaurant and hotel industry, including concept design, menu development, and tabletop design, as well as training for the front and the heart of the house.

Duck Crepes

6 servings

1½ cups flour

1 teaspoon sugar

1/8 teaspoon salt

3 eggs

1½ cups milk

2 tablespoons butter, melted

Goat Cheese and Duck Breast Filling (*see recipe that follows*)

Tomato Coulis (*see recipe that follows*)

Garnish: black kalamata olives; micro greens tossed in olive oil and lemon juice

Sift the dry ingredients into a bowl. Break the eggs into another bowl and mix until yolks and whites are blended. Make a hole in the middle of the dry ingredients and pour in beaten eggs.

Stir the flour mixture into the eggs little by little. Add the liquid a spoonful at a time and mix it in thoroughly before adding more liquid. When the mixture becomes easy to work, the remainder can be added in two portions. Add melted butter. Mix again, cover, and set aside for at least an hour.

Pour a generous tablespoon of butter into the pan to coat it with a thin layer of batter. When crepe is brown on the bottom, turn it and brown the other side.

Stuff crepes with filling; fold over with envelope seal. Heat in 350° oven for 10 minutes. Ladle coulis onto plate, place crepe on top with micro greens tossed in olive oil and lemon juice as garnish. Garnish sauce with black kalamata olives.

GOAT CHEESE AND DUCK BREAST FILLING

6 ounces goat cheese, softened

4 ounces marscapone cheese

12 ounces duck breast, diced

3 tablespoons sun dried tomatoes, chopped

2 tablespoons chives, chopped

In a bowl, mix all ingredients.

TOMATO COULIS

2 pounds ripe tomatoes, peeled and seeded

1 tablespoon olive oil

2 tablespoons minced shallots

1 garlic clove, minced

1 teaspoon red wine vinegar

1 tablespoon finely chopped fresh basil

1 ounce white truffle oil

salt and pepper

Quarter and core the tomatoes. Squeeze seeds and juice into sieve over small bowl, pressing to extract as much juice as possible. Discard seeds. Finely chop tomato pulp. Add to tomato juice. Heat olive oil in heavy large skillet over low heat.

Add shallots and garlic and cook until softened, stirring occasionally, about 5 minutes. Add tomatoes with their juice and boil until reduced to thick puree, stirring frequently, about 25 minutes. Stir in vinegar, truffle oil, and basil. Season with salt and pepper.

Dover Sole with Lobster and Asparagus, Spaghetti Squash, Pommes Gaufrette, and Citrus Beurre Blanc

6 servings

6 dover sole filets

9 ounces Maine lobster meat, cooked

18 asparagus spears, poached

Butter

Olive oil

Spaghetti Squash *(see recipe that follows)*

Pommes Gaufrette *(see recipe that follows)*

Citrus Beurre Blanc *(see recipe that follows)*

Season both sides of fish with salt and pepper. Roll the lobster and asparagus in the center and tie once in the middle with butcher's twine. Sauté fish in butter and olive oil. Reserve.

Toss cooked spaghetti squash in portion of beurre blanc sauce. Place in center of plate with potatoes on top. Then place fish on top of potatoes. Spoon sauce around plate and on top of fish.

SPAGHETTI SQUASH

1 large squash

Pierce the washed squash with a fork and roast for about one hour at 400°. Scoop out seeds and scrape with a fork to achieve spaghetti strands.

CITRUS BEURRE BLANC

Juice of 1 lemon

Juice of 1 lime

Juice of ½ orange

¼ cup white wine

1 tablespoon shallot, chopped

1 teaspoon garlic, chopped

12 ounces cold butter, cubed

3 tablespoons shredded zests of fruit

Sauté shallots and garlic in 1 ounce butter; add in all liquids and reduce by three-quarters. Whisk in remaining butter and finish with zest.

POMMES GAUFRETTE

1 large Yukon gold potato

Using a Japanese or French mandoline slicer, slice the potato alternately to achieve a crisscross cut. Pat dry and fry in peanut oil at 375° until golden brown. Reserve crisp lattice potato wafers and serve with the meal.

Warm Gingerbread with Caramel Sauce, Vanilla Crème Fraîche, and Raspberries

8 servings

½ cup butter

¾ cup sugar

1 cup molasses

2 eggs

2½ cups flour

1 teaspoon salt

2 teaspoons baking powder

½ teaspoon baking soda

1 teaspoon dry ginger

2 teaspoons cinnamon

½ teaspoon cloves

½ cup hot water

Vanilla crème fraîche

Caramel sauce

Garnish: fresh raspberries

Cream butter and sugar, then molasses. Beat in eggs one at a time. Sift flour, salt, baking powder, baking soda, and spices. Add to mixture alternately with hot water. Bake in greased 9-inch square pan or bundt pan for 40 minutes at 350°.

Slice warm gingerbread thinly on plate. Top with vanilla crème fraîche and drizzle with caramel sauce. Garnish with fresh raspberries.

There is only one thing that should be better dressed than you and that's your table!

Tuscany Revisited

Artist and friend Lise Peyser graces everything she touches with artistic sophistication and style.

Her call to have me design a table for a committee luncheon was a welcome gift to me, and thinking about all the beautiful dining areas in her Rancho Santa Fe, California, home where we could create a welcoming ambience, I let my imagination run rampant. I chose the pergola, with its white bougainvillea filtering the sunshine. What a lovely spot to entertain friends and committee members from San Diego Las Hermanas and transport them to Tuscany via the tabletop landscape!

Discussing future events and the group's annual fundraiser for St. Madeleine Sophie's Center is inspired in the shaded sunshine.

The Tabletop Landscape

An Italian garden statue stands ready to tend the garden and is surrounded by lush vegetables strewn casually on a floor-length Gaelic-leaf tablecloth.

Italian Foglia dishes by Vietri lend to the Tuscany atmosphere, and green flatware and stemware continue to bring the garden to the table.

Rusty-iron floral napkin rings, the color of rich earth, hold crisp white linen napkins crocheted with green edges and are the perfect contrast on the lush green setting.

Tangerine silk roses grow wild in the vegetable patch, the ideal spot to nestle place cards, and guests are delighted with the roses as favors to enjoy in their own homes.

Quick Tips

- A framed greeting welcoming your guests or announcing the organization you are entertaining is a lovely way to greet your friends and adds that special touch that everyone appreciates. A jewel of the table.
- Having silk vegetables and fruits in your arsenal of table decorations is a smart way to have a tabletop centerpiece at your fingertips.
- Keep your eye out for inexpensive statues at local home stores or garden shops. Enjoy them in your garden; then when you receive a phone call that unexpected guests are dropping by, put a statue on your table, surround it with moss and flowers or vegetables, and you have an instant masterpiece as a centerpiece!
- Elevating your statue on a pedestal or small box covered with cloth, moss, or flowers instantly elevates an inexpensive statue to a work of art.

"Make your centerpiece a Masterpiece."

Olga K.

TRATTORIA FANTASTICA

1731 India Street
San Diego, California

Joe Busalacchi
Owner and Executive Chef

Born in Porticillo, Sicily, Joe Busalacchi arrived in San Diego in 1966 with his parents and six brothers and sisters.

His Italian family loved to cook, to eat, and to share their recipes with friends and family, so it was natural for Joe to follow his heart after high school and learn the business from the ground up.

His dream was always to own his own restaurant and let the community enjoy his family's recipes. In 1982 he opened Casanova Pizzaria, followed by the upscale Busalacci's in 1986. Expansion to Little Italy came in 1995, with Trattoria Fantastica and Café Zucchero in 1996, Po Pazzo Bar and Grill in 2004, and Via Lago Trattoria in Eastlake, a suburb of San Diego, in 2007.

Chef Busalacchi's success as a restaurateur is simply his passion to serve delicious food and his ability to create restaurants that make customers feel at home, with a comfortable atmosphere and friendly service.

Menu

&ips; *Grilled Vegetable Salad with Balsamico Caper Vinaigrette*

&ips; *Dungeness Crab Angel Hair*

&ips; *Tiramisu*

Grilled Vegetable Salad with Balsamico Caper Vinaigrette

6 servings

3 cups mixed baby field greens

1 carrot, peeled and cut into julienne

1 pint red and yellow pear or cherry tomatoes

Olive oil

Salt and freshly ground black pepper

Grilled Vegetables (*see recipe that follows*)

Balsamico Caper Vinaigrette (*see recipe that follows*)

Garnish: tomatoes; carrot julienne

Toss the cooled grilled vegetables with a little olive oil and salt and pepper. Toss the mixed greens with enough vinaigrette to coat the leaves. Arrange grilled vegetables around the edge of the plate as desired and fill the center with the mixed greens. Garnish with tomatoes and carrot julienne. Crack a little black pepper over top and drizzle with just a touch of extra virgin olive oil.

GRILLED VEGETABLES

1 red bell pepper

1 yellow bell pepper

1 zucchini, ¼-inch cut

1 eggplant, ¼-inch cut

1 gold bar squash, ¼-inch cut

1 Portobello mushroom, peeled, cleaned of gills, and stemmed

Extra virgin olive oil

Salt and freshly ground black pepper to taste

Preheat gas or charcoal grill. Toss all vegetables in olive oil and some salt and pepper. Place bell peppers on grill and cook until burned on all sides. Then place in a bowl, cover with plastic film, and let steam for about 5 minutes. Grill the other vegetables until tender and allow to cool on a sheet pan. To finish the bell peppers, peel off the burned skin under cold running water; then cut in half and remove all seeds and white membrane. Slice the bell peppers and Portobello mushrooms into thin strips.

Chef's Note

- Try to turn each vegetable only once so you can achieve proper grill marks.

BALSAMICO CAPER VINAIGRETTE

½ cup extra virgin olive oil

2 tablespoons balsamic vinegar

1 tablespoon sherry vinegar

1 tablespoon capers

1½ teaspoons chopped anchovy fillets

½ teaspoon chopped garlic

½ teaspoon caper juice

Salt and freshly ground black pepper to taste

Puree all ingredients in a blender for 1 minute. Strain and set aside.

Dungeness Crab Angel Hair

6–8 servings

1 pound angel hair pasta

1 cup Dungeness crab meat

2 Roma tomatoes, diced

1 yellow tomato, diced

1 cup tomato sauce

½ cup clam juice

¼ cup dry white wine

3 tablespoons chopped parsley

8 jumbo scallops

1 shallot, finely chopped

1 clove garlic, finely chopped

Extra virgin olive oil

2 tablespoons unsalted butter

Salt and freshly ground white pepper

Heat a large pot of salted water to a boil. Heat a large sauté pan over medium-high heat and add 2 tablespoons extra virgin olive oil. Allow oil to heat and then add scallops and brown on one side. After about 1 minute, turn the scallops over and cook for a further 30 seconds. Remove the scallops from the pan and set aside.

Add the shallot and garlic to the pan and allow to soften, deglaze with white wine, and reduce by two-thirds. Add pasta to boiling water. While the pasta cooks, add the clam juice, chopped tomatoes, and crabmeat to the pan with shallot and garlic and heat. Add the tomato sauce and reduce all ingredients to the desired consistency.

When the pasta has cooked, strain and add to the sauce in the pan, along with the scallops and chopped parsley. Finish the pasta with the unsalted butter and season to taste with salt and pepper. Serve in warmed pasta bowls.

Chef's Note

- Do not shake the pan or move the scallops after putting them in the pan.

© Roman Pavlik. Shutterstock.

Tiramisu

8 servings

1 pound mascarpone

¼ cup sugar

1 cup heavy cream

6 tablespoons Marsala wine

24 imported Italian ladyfingers

1 cup brewed espresso, room temperature

½ cup shaved chocolate

Whisk together mascarpone, sugar, and wine in a large bowl. Whip cream in a chilled bowl with chilled beaters until soft peaks form. Fold the cream into the mascarpone mixture.

Dip half the ladyfingers in the espresso and put them in a single layer on the bottom of an 8-inch pan. Spread half the mascarpone mixture over the ladyfingers and sprinkle with shaved chocolate. Repeat with another layer.

Sprinkle shaved chocolate over the smooth mascarpone mixture. Refrigerate overnight before serving.

Turn an ordinary table into an extraordinary work of art!

The Art of the Table

Contemporary artist Gayle McInnes loves to entertain in her sleek, elegant penthouse and artist loft with the same creativity and passion she expresses in her art. Gayle's contemporary art takes center stage in her home, and when she invited me to help her plan a luncheon for the Art Alive committee from the San Diego Museum of Art, my creative juices went on overdrive.

Hosting the Art Alive committee called for a table meant to inspire her art-loving guests to even greater achievements at their annual spring fundraiser. Performance art on her luncheon table enveloped her guests with color and complimented the museum- quality art that surrounds visitors to her home.

Art is not always
what you see
But what an artist
makes others see.

The Tabletop Landscape

Oversized paintbrushes in art glass vases of orange, red, and blue-green sit at the end of a rectangular table, resting on a paint-splattered runner reminiscent of artist Jackson Pollock.

Art paper cut in different shapes serves as placemats, and white chargers resemble a simple frame for Rosenthal china.

Wood mannequins have fun hanging on vases dodging lemon leaf-covered pyramids, moss-covered squares, and round gerbera daisy balls that add a third dimension to the floral focal point. Multicolored tulip and martini glasses are part of the art on the table.

Watercolor porcelain pallets double as butter dishes and sit on top of colorful boxes filled with miniature water colors, mini paint brushes, and a small art book, which are the favors. Napkins, paint splattered, held by a contemporary metal napkin ring with a black enamel center and wood easels, hold Matisse postcards announcing each art aficionado's name.

This creative table will delight guests in your home, a museum, or an art gallery, art lovers or not.

Quick Tips

- Use ordinary paint cans from any local paint store in graduated sizes. Take off the paint labels and expose the aluminum cans. Mix paint with paint sticks and drip primary colors all around the sides and let the paint dry.
- Set the paint sticks aside and let dry. Empty the paint cans into other containers and save for another project.
- Fill paint cans with water and fill with colorful spring bouquets. Nestle the paint sticks and paintbrushes randomly in the flower arrangement to show your artistic flair.
- Create your focal point at the end of a rectangular table instead of the center, and you can go as high as you want with your art piece.
- Make artist Andy Warhol the center of attention on your next art table by using Campbell soup cans reminiscent of his famous painting, filled with flowers and small paintbrushes to make an easy artistic centerpiece.

WATERS FINE CATERING

1105 West Morena Blvd.
San Diego, California

Mary Kay Waters
Executive Director and Owner

Andrew Ryland Spurgin
Executive Director and Chef

For over twelve years, Mary Kay Waters and Chef Andrew Spurgin have produced outstanding culinary creations for the most discerning clientele.

Mary Kay received her BS in nutrition at the University of Maryland and her AOS at the Culinary Institute of America. She also holds a degree from L'Academie de Cuisine under White House Executive Pastry Chef Roland Mesnier.

Andrew has built his culinary career spanning three decades. He has designed menus and events honoring such dignitaries as U.S. presidents Bill Clinton and Ronald Reagan, former Soviet president Mikhail Gorbachev, former Israeli prime minister Shimon Peres, former California governors Pete Wilson and Gray Davis, and Martha Stewart. Regular clients include Tiffany & Co., Cartier, Merrill Lynch, Aston Martin, Bloomingdale's and Nissan Design.

Andrew's events have been featured in numerous local and national magazines and on television. He lectures regularly on the sustainability of food and entertaining. Andrew was voted national finalist (1999, 2001) and 2003 Caterer of the Year by *Event Solutions* magazine. Chef Spurgin also has been honored with an invitation to cook at the famed James Beard House in New York City.

Menu

❧ *Peekytoe Crab Timbale with Mango and Avocado*

❧ *Grilled Wild Alaskan Salmon and White Peaches with Wildflower Honey*

❧ *Lavender Panna Cotta with Honeyed Tangerine and Berries*

Peekytoe Crab Timbale with Mango and Avocado

4 servings

¾ pound Peekytoe crab meat, gently pulled apart*

¼ teaspoon tangerine zest, finely chopped

1 teaspoon celery leaves, finely chopped

½ teaspoon chives, finely snipped

2 teaspoons mayonnaise

1 tablespoon plus ½ teaspoon lemon olive oil**

1 (375-ml) bottle Port, slowly reduced to 1½ ounces

1 avocado, chopped into fine cubes

1 mango, chopped into fine cubes

½ tablespoon sea salt, slightly ground

Garnish: 3 bachelor button blossoms

*Peekytoe crab available from Browne Trading, (800) 944-7848 or www. brownetrading.com.

**Flavored O brand olive oils available at specialty stores or online at www. ooliveoil.com.

Lightly toss crab with tangerine zest, celery leaves, chives, mayonnaise, and ½ teaspoon lemon olive oil. Check for seasonings and refrigerate.

Place crab mixture in timbale mold (or you can use a small paper cup) and invert onto plate. Use fine-tipped squirt bottle to drizzle plate with reduced Port. Place small pile of cubed avocado and mango next to timbale and sprinkle with sea salt. Drizzle and dot the plate with olive oil from a fine-tipped squirt bottle. Garnish with bachelor button blossoms.

Grilled Wild Alaskan Salmon and White Peaches with Wildflower Honey

4 servings

Make sure to use a very clean grill! Prefire grill with hardwood charcoal to high heat and season the grill with grapeseed oil several times so fish will not stick. You are ready to grill when you cannot hold your hand over the grill for more than a few seconds.

1½ pounds wild Alaskan salmon filet, skin on

1 tablespoon sea salt

2 tablespoons grapeseed oil

1 teaspoon blood orange olive oil*

1 teaspoon ruby grapefruit olive oil*

½ teaspoon Tellicherry peppercorns, medium ground

3 heads Belgian endive

2 bunches watercress

White Peaches with Wildflower Honey *(see recipe that follows)*

Garnishes: 1/8 teaspoon orange zest, finely chopped; ½ teaspoon chives, finely snipped; ½ teaspoon parsley, finely chopped

*Flavored O brand olive oils available at specialty stores or online at www. ooliveoil.com.

Cut salmon into four portions. Lightly salt skin side. Sear skin side down on grill for 2 minutes or until crust forms. Remove from grill, brush salmon with grapeseed oil; sprinkle with peppercorns and sea salt and return to grill, meat side down. Check for doneness (approximately 4–5 minutes depending on thickness of salmon). Remove from grill.

Julienne the Belgian endive and toss with watercress. Add a hint of flavored olive oils and a pinch of sea salt and pepper.

Place salad on plate, top with salmon, drizzle lightly with flavored olive oils. Lean grilled peaches on salmon and top with chives, parsley, and orange zest.

WHITE PEACHES WITH WILDFLOWER HONEY

2 white tree-ripened peaches
1 tablespoon wildflower honey

Remove stones and cut peaches into four sections each. Toss peaches in a little flavored olive oils, sprinkle with peppercorns, and grill for 30 seconds on each side. Remove from grill and drizzle with wildflower honey.

Lavender Panna Cotta with Honeyed Tangerine and Berries

4 servings

1/3 cup sugar
21/3 cups whole milk
2/3 cup whipping cream
1 teaspoon pure vanilla extract
1 packet gelatin
1 teaspoon Lavender Cream (see recipe that follows)
3 tablespoons wildflower honey
1 pint assorted berries
2 tangerines, segmented

Place the sugar, whole milk, and whipping cream in a heavy saucepan and bring to a boil. Remove from heat. Stir in the vanilla

and gelatin. Slowly add the lavender cream to taste. Start with about a teaspoon and add more as desired.

Cool only slightly and pour into six martini glasses (or other unique serving vessel), two-thirds to top. Refrigerate until set, approximately 4 hours. To serve, top with berries and tangerine segments and drizzle with the best wildflower honey you can get your hands on!

LAVENDER CREAM

1 cup whipping cream
1/3 cup dry lavender buds and petals

Place whipping cream and dry lavender buds and petals in a saucepan and bring to a simmer. Simmer about 5 minutes, tasting periodically. Flavor should be infused but never bitter; lavender can vary greatly in its intensity. Strain cream through a fine sieve and cool.

Like a welcome hug, the dining room welcomes you and reminds you how it feels to be exactly where you're sup~posed to be, sharing food, fun, and frivolity with the people you love.

Autumn Harvest

Autumn weather brings crisp mornings, falling leaves, and in California the sun warms the afternoon so grandchildren can play a game of touch football before the professionals take over on national TV. The older generation sits by the warmth of the hearth doing what families always do: recapture memories of family far from home, share amusing stories of summer vacations, and make plans to gather the family for the holidays.

Sunday supper in the fall—with soup simmering on the stove, chicken baking in the oven, and a fire burning brightly in the fireplace—is a warm setting your family and friends relish and love to be a part of. This tradition of gathering family to spend time together sharing precious moments and recipes is what must be passed down to children and grandchildren in order to preserve the heritage we want to pass down to generations to come.

The Tabletop Landscape

A porcelain pumpkin soup tureen is center stage, surrounded by a medley of harvest vegetables that includes artichokes, corn, eggplants, squash, peppers, and tomatoes. Rusty wire chickens stroll through the vegetables and are surrounded by autumn reeds, weeds, and stalks of wheat.

A carpet of autumn leaves blankets the table, a colorful background for gold-rimmed chargers, white Wedgewood china, ornate crystal, and gold goblets. Gold flatware enhances the setting.

Napkins in fall colors are held by elegant gold tassels. Votives wrapped with see-through ribbon and embellished with orange autumn leaves glow brightly on the table and highlight the place cards. The country French ladder-back chairs wrapped with stalks of wheat and held in place with gold cording complete this fall tablescape.

Quick Tips

- Your dining chairs are a natural extension of your tabletop landscape. Decorating the back of every chair is a spectacular and unexpected way to highlight the setting. Decorate the backs of all the chairs or only one chair to honor a special guest.

- A wreath or floral spray that follows the color scheme of your tablescape attaches to the back of your chair with wire ribbon at both the top and bottom of the chair for stability

- A birthday, graduation, anniversary, or welcome home greeting attached to a 10-inch ribbon sash and tied around the chair is as easy as 1-2-3 and will garner you no less than three compliments!

JONNA D. TALBOTT
Private Executive Chef
San Diego, California

After graduating from the California Culinary Academy in San Diego, California, in 1998, Jonna Talbott became a private caterer and personal chef to clients who appreciate the quality of food and creative menus she consistently prepares.

As chef assistant to visiting chefs at Macy's School of Cooking, Jonna was able to develop her own style of teaching, which led to teaching classes for *Bon Appétit* magazine. In 2003, the Montage Resort and Spa in Laguna Beach approached Jonna to test recipes for three of their chefs, and subsequently she worked with Montage to revise recipes so that they could be shared with the general public.

One of Jonna's strongest passions is teaching children about the joy of creativity through cooking. She has taught cooking camps for young chefs and believes in starting children in the kitchen when they are as young as two.

Jonna is currently public relations/event planner at Macy's Home Store in San Diego and takes great pleasure in hosting famous chefs at Macy's state-of-the-art School of Cooking.

Menu

 • *Harvest Sweet Potato Soup*

 • *Phyllo-Wrapped Dill Chicken*

 • *Orange-Scented Green Beans*

 • *Lemon Chiffon Tart with Raspberry Coulis*

Harvest Sweet Potato Soup

8 servings

- 2 shallots, finely chopped
- 3 tablespoons butter
- 1 large glove garlic, finely minced
- 2 teaspoon curry powder
- 2 large sweet potatoes (approximately 2 pounds)
- 4 cups chicken stock (preferably home-made)
- 2 large Granny Smith apples, peeled, cored, and cut into 1-inch cubes
- 1/8 teaspoon cayenne pepper (optional)
- *Garnish:* Crème fraîche or sour cream; finely chopped chives or Toasted Pecans (*see recipe that follows*)

Sauté the shallots in butter until soft, about 3 minutes. Add garlic and sauté for about 30 seconds. Add the curry powder and stir well. Add the sweet potatoes and chicken stock. Simmer for about 15 minutes.

Add the apples and continue to cook until the potatoes and apples are fork tender, about 10–15 minutes.

Using a slotted spoon, transfer small amounts of the potatoes and apples to a food processor or blender. Puree with some of the liquid until smooth. Transfer to a saucepan. Repeat this process with remaining potatoes. If needed, add additional chicken stock. Consistency should be medium thick.

Simmer soup an additional 5 minutes or until hot. Add the cayenne pepper (if using) and the cream. Heat an additional 2–3 minutes. Season to taste with salt and pepper.

Garnish with crème fraiche or sour cream and sprinkle with finely chopped chives or toasted pecans.

Toasted Pecans

¾ cup pecans

In a small skillet, toast the pecans, stirring occasionally for about 10 minutes. Pecans should be golden brown and fragrant. Allow to cool and chop finely. Pecans can be made up to two days in advance. Store airtight until ready to use.

CRÈME FRAÎCHE

- 1 cup heavy cream
- ¼ cup Buttermilk
- 1 tablespoon lemon juice

Mix 1 cup heavy cream, ¼ cup buttermilk and 1 tablespoon lemon juice. Cover and let sit at room temperature 6-8 hours, then refrigerate.

Crème fraîche is great for cooking because of its rich flavor and stability—it doesn't break when heated, unlike sour cream.

Phyllo-Wrapped Dill Chicken

4 servings

- 1 tablespoon butter
- 1 tablespoon olive oil
- 2 gloves garlic, minced
- 2–3 pounds boneless, skinless chicken breasts (about 4 chicken breasts), roughly chopped
- ¾ cup finely chopped green onion
- ¾ cup mayonnaise
- ¾ cup freshly grated Asiago cheese or Parmesean cheese
- 2 tablespoons lemon juice, freshly squeezed

1 tablespoon fresh dill
    (or 1 teaspoon dried dill)

¼ teaspoon sesame oil

½ teaspoon salt

½ teaspoon freshly cracked pepper

1 pound box phyllo dough

Clarified butter

¾ cup plain bread crumbs

Marsala Wine Sauce (*see recipe that follows*)

Garnish: freshly grated Asiago or Parmesan
    cheese; finely chopped parsley

Preheat oven to 350°. Place butter and olive oil in a large sauté pan over medium heat. When butter melts, add the chicken and garlic. Sauté about 5 minutes or until the chicken is no longer pink. Allow to cool about 15 minutes.

When chicken is cool enough to handle, place in a food processor equipped with a metal blade. Working in batches, pulse until chicken is about the size of a dime. Transfer to a large bowl. To the chicken add the green onions, cheese, mayonnaise, lemon juice, dill, sesame oil, salt, and pepper. Gently stir to combine.

Line a sheet pan with parchment paper. Unwrap phyllo dough and cover with a clean damp towel (this helps prevent the dough from drying out). Working on a large cutting board, place three sheets of phyllo dough on board. Think of phyllo dough as a book: fold 2 sheets back halfway and brush with clarified butter. Cover with the next sheet and brush with butter. Fold the third sheet back into original position. Repeat with the other side of the "book." Butter the top layer of phyllo dough. Sprinkle with breadcrumbs.

About 2 inches from the middle of the short edge of the phyllo dough, place about one-fourth of the chicken mixture.

Cover with one-third of the dough using the longer edge and brush with clarified butter. (Don't worry if the dough does not completely cover the chicken, as the other third of the dough should cover the balance of the chicken mixture.) Next, fold over the other third. Brush with clarified butter. Sprinkle with bread crumbs. Beginning at the end that contains the chicken, "roll" the phyllo dough, brushing each fold with butter. When you reach the end, brush butter over the entire packet and place on the parchment-lined sheet pan. Repeat with remaining chicken.

At this point, chicken packets can be covered with plastic wrap and refrigerated until ready to bake. Can be made 6 hours in advance. Remove from refrigerator when you begin to preheat the oven.

Bake, covered, at 350° for about 20 minutes, or until golden brown. To serve, make a pool of wine sauce on each plate. Depending on the size of your rolls, serve whole or cut them in half. Place on top of sauce. If desired, sprinkle with additional cheese and parsley.

MARSALA WINE SAUCE

2 tablespoons butter

2 shallots, finely chopped

¼ pound mushrooms, thinly sliced

3 tablespoons flour

1 cup chicken stock

¼ cup dry Marsala wine

¼ cup dry white wine

Salt and pepper to taste.

In a medium sauté pan, melt the butter, add the shallots and mushrooms and sauté until shallots are translucent. Add flour and cook together a few minutes to form a roux (paste). Do not allow to brown. Add the chicken stock and whisk together until smooth and lump free. Continue to reduce the sauce until it is of a medium consistency. Add salt and pepper to taste. Sauce can be made 2 hours in advance and reheated over low heat.

Orange-Scented Green Beans

4 servings

2 teaspoons salt

1 pound fresh green beans, ends snapped or trimmed

2 tablespoons butter

Zest of one orange

1 teaspoon orange olive oil* (or to taste)

*Flavored O brand olive oils available at specialty stores or online at www. ooliveoil.com.

Bring a large pot of water to a boil and add the salt. Add the green beans and blanch just until done, about 5 minutes. Do not overcook. Drain and immerse in an ice bath to halt the cooking process. Drain the green beans and set aside. (This step could be done several hours ahead of time. Refrigerate the green beans and bring to room temperature before proceeding.)

Melt the butter in a large sauté pan over medium heat. Add the zest and sauté until fragrant and butter is golden brown, about 2–3 minutes. Add the green beans and toss to coat with the butter. Add the flavored olive oil and toss once more.

Lemon Chiffon Tart with Raspberry Coulis

10 servings

3 eggs, separated

1/8 teaspoon salt

½ cup sugar

¼ cup lemon juice, freshly squeezed

1 teaspoon lemon zest

1 cup heavy cream

2 cups shortbread cookies, crushed

4 tablespoons melted butter

2 tablespoon sugar

1 tablespoon Limoncello (optional)

Garnish: Raspberry Coulis (see recipe that follows); raspberries or strawberries; mint

Beat egg yolks, salt, and ½ cup sugar in double boiler. Add lemon juice and zest. As mixture begins to thicken, add Limoncello (if using), cook until thickened and coats the back of a spoon. Chill until cool, about 45–60 minutes.

Preheat oven to 350°. While the lemon mixture is cooling, prepare the crust. Combine the crushed cookies with the melted butter in a small bowl. Butter a 9-inch springform pan and press crumb mixture over the bottom. Bake about 20 minutes or until golden brown. Allow to cool before filling.

Beat egg whites until stiff and add 2 tablespoons sugar. Whip the cream until firm. Fold the whipped cream and lemon mixture into the egg whites. Continue to fold until the lemon mixture is completely incorporated. Pour mixture into spring form pan. Smooth the top. Cover with plastic wrap. Freeze until firm. Can be made two days in advance. To serve, decorate dessert plates attractively with the coulis and garnish with berries and mint.

RASPBERRY COULIS

Yield: about 1 cup

1 (10 ounce) package frozen raspberries in syrup

2 tablespoons sugar

1 teaspoon fresh lemon juice

1 teaspoon Chambord (optional)

Puree raspberries, sugar, and lemon juice in a food processor. Pour mixture through a fine strainer into a bowl, forcing the mixture through the strainer with the back of a spoon. If desired, add the Chambord. Can be made up to three days in advance. Store covered in the refrigerator. (For an easy way to store, pour into plastic squeeze bottle.)

Chef's Note:

- Frozen strawberries may be substituted for raspberries.

© Neil Webster. Shutterstock.

© Caroline J Clarke. Shutterstock.

Everything that lives in water

is seductive.

"Unexpected guests should always be welcome!"

Olga K.

Guess Who's Coming to Dinner

The most pleasant hours of our life are connected with some memory of the table.

—Charles Pierre Monselet

The Koi Pond

*W*here water serenely trickles into a Koi pond and golden fish cut gracefully through the water is my neighbor Sandy Canfield's favorite place in her garden.

Sandy's luscious garden and her Koi pond inspired me to create a dinner retreat where guests could share in a tea ceremony and then enjoy mouthwatering Asian fusion cuisine in a quiet Zen-like retreat. The perfect setting to celebrate her mother's birthday!

Fortune cookies—with good fortunes only—are the order of the day for Sandy's guests at her dinner party.

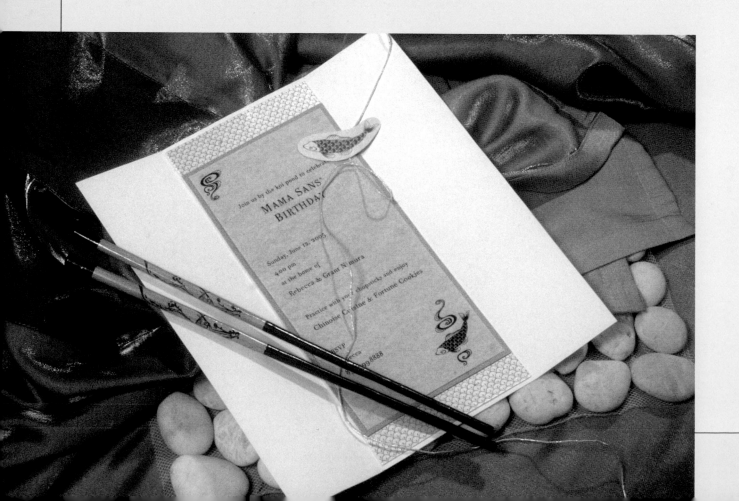

The Tabletop Landscape

Celebrating any special occasion can be exhilarating when you hold the party in a surprise location.

An Asian-inspired cocktail table placed by the Koi pond immediately sets the stage for an exciting venue to celebrate a special occasion. White rock placemats surround an oversized golden ceramic Koi fish balancing a rattan-trimmed glass bowl on his back. In the bowl, small red and gold fish swim happily among floating white orchids.

White orchid napkin rings hold luxurious silk napkins and lie next to aqua and sea green pottery-ware that compliments the seaweed-shaped branch flatware and enamel chopsticks.

Iridescent salmon silk pillows are a warm contrast to the blue water and gleam in the late afternoon sunlight, inviting guests to sit and be comfortable.

Japanese fans and porcelain fortune cookies by a Laguna Beach artist filled with good fortunes are favors for guests to take home as a remembrance of the evening.

Quick Tips

- Invitations for an Asian-themed dinner party can be written on a Japanese fan, or send a fortune cookie in a Chinese take-out container with the invitation written on rice paper.
- Japanese teapots filled with chopsticks and a single orchid, ikebana style, make a great centerpiece.
- Chinese take-out containers can be used as vases. Fill with flowers and add chopsticks.

Menu

≈ *Ahi Poke on Crispy Wontons*

≈ *Anise BBQ Ribs in Chile Orange Glaze*

≈ *Tiger Shrimp and Rice Noodle Pot Stickers with Microgreens and Fish Essence*

≈ *Jonah Crab Cakes with Asian Tartar Sauce*

≈ *Zatar-Dusted Maine Sea Scallops with Yellow Corn Pancakes*

ROPPONGI LA JOLLA

875 Prospect Street
La Jolla, California

Stephen B. Window
Executive Chef

Memorable dining is all about exploration and adventure, an experience embodied at Roppongi in La Jolla, California.

At Roppongi, exotic flavors from throughout the Far East are married with classic European techniques, resulting in a cuisine that celebrates Southern California's multiethnic heritage.

British-born executive chef Stephen B. Window attended culinary school near his hometown of Manchester, England, and embarked on a career that would take him to acclaimed restaurants around the world, including the Stanneylands Hotel, where he won Young Chef of the Year honors.

Stephen joined Sami Ladeki, the successful and dynamic restaurateur, in 1998 and opened La Jolla's Roppongi, where both his love of classic culinary traditions and his appreciation for the diverse flavors of the Pacific have been allowed to flourish.

During Stephen's tenure at Roppongi, the restaurant has won many awards and he has received top honors, including the Culinary Institute of America's Chef of the Year 2001 and Critic's Choice for Best Chef of the Year by *San Diego Magazine*. Chef Window also has served as featured chef at the James Beard House—an honor all chefs dream of—not once but twice!

Ahi Poke on Crispy Wontons

4 servings

1 pound fresh ahi tuna (grade 1)

½ cup soy sauce

¼ cup chopped green onions

1 tablespoon sesame oil

½ tablespoon toasted sesame seeds

½ tablespoon crushed red pepper

8 wonton wrappers

1 cup peanut oil

Garnish: 4 ounces peashoots

Remove any blood lines from ahi. Dice fish very small. Mix in a bowl with green onions, sesame oil, toasted sesame seeds, crushed red pepper, and soy sauce. Cook wonton wrappers in peanut oil until crispy. Allow to cool. Place poke on wonton wrappers and garnish with peashoots.

Anise BBQ Ribs in Chile Orange Glaze

4 servings

2 pounds baby back pork ribs

8 sticks anise

4 bay leaves

2 ounces garlic

10 black peppercorns

2 cups orange juice

Water to cover

Chile Orange Glaze (*see recipe that follows*)

Garnish: orange slices

Place ribs in braising pan with ingredients. Bring to a boil and simmer until tender. Allow to cool. Cut into individual ribs. Marinate in glaze 24 hours. Cook on grill; garnish with orange slices.

CHILE ORANGE GLAZE

1 tablespoon olive oil

2 tablespoons shallots

4 tablespoons chopped garlic

2 tablespoons fresh ginger

½ jalapeno pepper, sliced

¼ red bell pepper, diced

½ bunch scallions

4 Szechwan peppercorns

1 fresh tomato, diced

2 oranges, diced

1 cup sake

1 cup mirin

2 tablespoons soy sauce

2 tablespoon chicken stock

2 tablespoons water

1 cup sugar

1 cup orange juice

Heat oil. Add shallot, garlic, ginger, jalapeno, bell pepper, and scallions. Stir. Add tomato, oranges, sake, mirin, and soy sauce, peppercorns, water, chicken stock, and orange juice. Reduce to glaze.

© Cyril Hou. Shutterstock.

" A lively splash of color is instant gratification!"

Olga K.

Tiger Shrimp and Rice Noodle Pot Stickers with Microgreens and Fish Essence

4 servings

½ package rice stick noodles (available at Asian groceries), cooked and drained

16 Gyoza wrappers (pot sticker wrappers)

Egg wash (1 egg plus 1 tablespoon water)

Shrimp Filling (see recipe that follows)

Vegetable oil for frying

Fish Essence (see recipe that follows)

Garnish: microgreens

Brush each wrapper with egg wash and add a spoonful of shrimp filling into the center of wrapper. Fold in half and pinch edges until completely sealed.

In large sauté pan, heat vegetable oil over medium-high heat. Gently lay the pot stickers in the pan and sauté for about 5 minutes, until the bottoms begin to brown. Turn over and cook until pot stickers are browned evenly on both sides.

Sprinkle 2 tablespoons of water into the pan and quickly cover the pan. Let pot stickers steam for another 5 minutes. Remove pan from heat until ready to serve. Garnish with microgreens and serve with Fish Essence.

SHRIMP FILLING

1½ pounds shrimp (16–20 count), cleaned and deveined

1 tablespoon ginger

1 tablespoon garlic

¼ cup chopped mint

2 cups bok choy, finely sliced

1 tablespoon olive oil

Salt and pepper

Heat olive oil in nonstick pan. Add ginger and garlic. Cook for 2–3 minutes. Add bok choy, chives, and mint. Remove from pan and strain through cheesecloth until cool, squeezing out excess moisture. Place mixture into a bowl and set aside. Place clean shrimp in food processor and puree. To the bowl with the bok choy mixture add pureed shrimp and cooked rice noodles and mix together. Add salt and pepper to taste.

FISH ESSENCE

2 pounds lobster shells

1 cup onions, finely chopped

1 cup carrots, finely chopped

½ cup lemongrass, split

2 bay leaves

1 cup tomato paste

1 cup heavy cream

½ cup butter

4 cups water

Place lobster and shrimp shells in oven; roast to a golden brown color. Heat a heavy nonstick pan. Add ¼ cup butter and then the vegetables. Cook 4–5 minutes, stirring to brown evenly.

Add roasted lobster shells, tomato paste, lemongrass and bay leaf. Cover with water and bring to boil. Simmer 45 minutes.

Strain and reduce stock to 1/3 original volume. Add heavy cream. Reduce by half again. Strain. Season with salt and pepper to taste. Add remaining butter, cubed, whisking thoroughly.

Jonah Crab Cakes with Asian Tartar Sauce

4 servings

1 pound Jonah or Dungeness crab

½ cup finely diced carrots

½ cup finely diced onions

½ cup finely diced celery

2 tablespoons finely minced garlic

¼ cup mayonnaise

¼ cup heavy cream

Salt

White pepper

1 ounce Thai basil

1 teaspoon finely chopped dill

1 teaspoon finely chopped chives

¾ cup panko bread crumbs

½ cup flour

2 eggs

4 tablespoons butter

½ cup peanut oil

Asian Tartar Sauce (*see recipe that follows*)

Heat nonstick pan. Add butter and garlic. Sauté. Add onions, celery, and carrots. Cook without darkening over medium heat. Add basil and chives. Remove from pan and place on tray to cool.

Squeeze excess moisture from crab and place crab in bowl. Add vegetables, mayonnaise, salt, and pepper. Heat heavy cream. Reduce by half and allow to cool. Form mixture into 16 small rounds. Dip into flour, egg, and panko bread crumbs. In shallow pan, fry cakes in peanut oil for approximately 3–4 minutes. Remove and place on absorbent paper. Serve with tartar sauce.

ASIAN TARTAR SAUCE

2 cups mayonnaise

½ cup finely chopped red onion

¼ cup capers, strained and finely chopped

Juice from 1 lemon

¼ cup chopped parsley

½ cup seaweed salad

½ cucumber, peeled and julienned

1 teaspoon fish sauce

Shichimi spice and salt to taste

Place mayonnaise in bowl. Add lemon juice, salt, and Shichimi spice to taste. Add onions and remaining ingredients. Combine.

Zatar-Dusted Maine Sea Scallops with Yellow Corn Pancakes

4 servings

1 tablespoon zatar spice

1½ teaspoons sesame seeds

1½ teaspoons curry powder

1½ teaspoons salt

1½ teaspoons black pepper

4 tablespoons olive oil

4 tablespoons butter

8 jumbo sea scallops

½ cup mayonnaise

¼ cup chukka salad (seasoned Japanese seaweed salad)

Yellow Corn Pancakes
   (*see recipe that follows*)

Garnish: ¼ cup tiny greens; 2 tablespoons minced chives

Combine sesame seeds, zatar, and curry powder. Dust clean fresh scallops with spices. Heat nonstick pan. Add butter.

Cook scallops medium rare over medium heat.

Combine mayonnaise and finely chopped chukka salad. Place on top of pancakes. Top with scallops. Garnish with chives and/or greens.

YELLOW CORN PANCAKES

2 tablespoons butter

2 eggs

¾ cup milk

1 cup corn meal

½ cup all-purpose flour

1 tablespoon white sugar

2 teaspoons baking powder

1 cup yellow corn puree or fresh corn cooked in fish or chicken stock, drained

Combine eggs, milk, and sugar. Add sifted flour, baking powder, and melted butter. Strain. Add pureed corn or fresh corn. Cook in small rounds, ½ inch larger than scallops.

The gift of good company and the sharing of delicious food is cause for celebration.

© 7122279 6837. Shutterstock.

The Geisha and the Samurai

*B*arbara Cipranic was my interior design partner at Macy's Home Store in San Diego, California, and although our styles are diametrically opposed, I always admired her flair for the contemporary style she specializes in and the monochromatic colors she lives with.

A call to say that two of our favorite business associates, Jim White and Debbie Young in San Francisco, were coming to San Diego to work in our design studio gave Barbara and me the opportunity to entertain Jim and Debbie on our home turf. We divided the responsibilities. Barbara took care of the menu and food, and I designed the invitation and the tabletop landscape.

The choices were easy. Our friend Mineko Moreno was available to do her Asian magic with food, and I had just purchased a complete set of oriental dishes that would blend into Barbara's dining room.

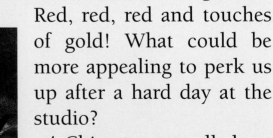

Red, red, red and touches of gold! What could be more appealing to perk us up after a hard day at the studio?

A Chinese gong called our guests to the table, where we shared delicious food and interior design ideas and made plans for buying trips to China and Japan.

The Tabletop Landscape

Great things happen in small spaces. Don't be fooled into thinking you need a mansion in order to entertain. You may not be able to entertain fifty at a time, but this table for four shows what you can accomplish in a small space.

The vases copy ancient red robes in three different shapes and sizes and are the unusual containers for three different elements. Long bamboo wrapped with reeds, red grass shoots, and spiral red reeds with fresh grass and red zinnias were the focal point at the end of the rectangular table. (Who says you can't sit across from each other?)

Don Janais's interior design showroom provided sunsilk fabrics in red and gold, each with a different Asian motif, that form a river of silk down the center of the table and also wrap around parson chairs as obis.

Candles float on the silk river in small red lacquer containers, grounded by white sand, small river rocks, and Chinese coins for good luck. Faux Raku plates, bowls, and saki cups sit on Japanese trays, with chopstick holders and chopsticks resting gently on the pyramid.

Napkins in red polished cotton with celery green edges are held by dragonfly napkin rings, and oriental fans are both a favor and the place card.

Quick Tips

- Candles create a magical aura at a dinner table, but make sure to use unscented candles so as not to interfere with the aromas of the food.
- A table runner down the center of the table creates instant atmosphere and allows you

- Use runners perpendicular to the length of the table, letting them drape dramatically to the floor and using them as place mats or tablecloth.

MINEKO TAKANE MORENO

Private Executive Chef
6795 Via Casa Del Sol
Carlsbad, California

Mineko Moreno is author of *Sushi for Dummies* and is cofounder of Personal Style, a fashion décor and party design consulting service. Mineko is also currently on staff and teaching at Macy's School of Cooking, William Sonoma, Sur La Table, Great News Cooking School, San Diego Culinary Institute, Kitchen Witch Gourmet Shop, and the Balboa Park Food and Wine School.

Mineko has given demonstrations about the art of Japanese cooking on KPBS, *The Lounge*; NBC, *Channel 39 Morning News*; CBS, *Sun Up San Diego*; and at the *San Diego Home/Garden Lifestyles* show.

Mineko's skills as a cooking teacher and as a professional flower designer bring beauty, harmony, and a sense of balance to all her preparations. She believes that to prepare any dish well you must consider the four senses of sight, smell, taste, and touch from the moment you plan the dish to its completion and presentation. Chef Moreno knows that cooking and eating well are an important part of life, worthy of great care, time, and attention.

Menu

❧ *Chilled Sake*

❧ *Japanese Consommé with Egg, Enoki Mushrooms, and Scallion Garnish*

❧ *Grilled Marinated Salmon with Spicy Daikon*

❧ *Mixed Greens Salad with Ginger Rice Vinegar Dressing*

❧ *Fresh Green Peas Rice*

❧ *Green Tea Ice Cream*

❧ *Green Tea*

Japanese Consommé with Egg, Enoki Mushrooms, and Scallion Garnish

4–6 servings

4 cups water

1 4-inch square of dried kelp (dashi konbu)

1 dried shiitake mushroom

2 cups dried bonito flakes (katsuobushi)

½ teaspoon salt, or to taste

1 teaspoon light color Japanese soy sauce (usukuchi shoyu)

1 teaspoon sake

2 eggs, beaten

1 package (3.5 ounce) enoki mushrooms, roots cut off

1 scallion, thinly sliced

Garnish: 4 small pieces of lemon peel

Pour 4 cups of water in a pot. Wipe dried kelp with a moist towel and rinse dried shiitake mushroom. Add both to the pot and bring water to a boil slowly over medium heat to bring out the flavor of the kelp and shiitake. When the water starts to boil, take out the kelp but leave the shiitake in the stock and add a small amount of water to stop the boiling. Then add the dried bonito flakes. When the stock comes back to a boil, turn off the heat. Wait a few minutes; then strain the stock with a fine mesh strainer.

Warm the stock and season with salt; mix well to dissolve salt and add soy sauce and sake. Bring the seasoned stock to the boiling point and pour the beaten eggs into the soup in a circular pattern, over chopsticks to create a steady stream. Add the enoki mushrooms and scallions and turn off the heat. Pour the soup into individual bowls and garnish with lemon peel. Serve immediately.

Chef's Note

- When pouring beaten eggs into the soup, pour over chopsticks and in a circular pattern.
- Do not mix soup immediately after eggs are added to the soup or the soup will become cloudy.

Grilled Marinated Salmon with Spicy Daikon

4 servings

4 (approximately 5½-ounce) slices salmon filet with skin

¼ cup Japanese soy sauce (shoyu)

¼ cup mirin

¼ cup sake

1 tablespoon ginger juice

Spicy Daikon (*see recipe that follows*)

Garnish: 4 lemon wedges

Slice each salmon filet into 2 to 3 pieces. Combine shoyu, mirin, sake, and ginger juice in a shallow dish and marinate the salmon for about 30 minutes. (Periodically flip the fish to marinate both sides.)

Place a wire rack on a baking sheet covered with aluminum foil. Place the marinated fish skin side down on the rack and broil both sides until the fish is almost done; then brush with the marinade 2–3 times while finishing broiling. Serve with daikon and garnish with lemon wedges.

SPICY DAIKON

¼ cup grated daikon

Japanese 7-spice (Shichimi togarashi) to taste

- You may cook the marinade over medium-high heat for 4–5 minutes and serve on the side.
- This may also be done over a stovetop grill or barbecue. The fish can burn easily. Grill or broil over medium heat or place the baking sheet away from the heat. Serve with steamed or boiled vegetables.
- Fish may be served hot or at room temperature.

Mixed Greens Salad with Ginger Rice Vinegar Dressing

4–6 servings

5 cups mixed greens

1 cup thinly sliced cucumber

½ cup good quality rice vinegar

1½ tablespoons sugar

1 teaspoon light color Japanese soy sauce (usukuchi shoyu)

½ teaspoon minced fresh ginger

Wash and soak mixed greens in ice water for 10–15 minutes or until crisp. Drain and spin dry.

In the meantime, combine vinegar, sugar, soy sauce, and minced ginger. Mix well to dissolve sugar completely.

Place prepared mixed greens and cucumber slices on individual plates and pour dressing over and around the salad. Serve immediately.

Chef's Note
- For serving chilled, place the salad in the refrigerator before pouring the dressing.

Fresh Green Peas Rice

4–6 servings

This is a very tasty and simple way to enjoy fresh peas in season.

3 cups short - or medium-grain white rice

3–3½ cups water

1½ cups fresh green peas

2 teaspoons salt (1 teaspoon for cooking rice, 1 teaspoon for peas)

3 tablespoons sake

Wash rice in cold tap water until water almost runs clear (about 6–8 times); then drain. Soak the washed rice with the measured water (water level should be about ¾–1 inch above the rice) in a rice cooker for about 1 hour. Add sake and 1 teaspoon salt. Start the rice cooker.

Place the fresh peas in a bowl. Add 1 teaspoon salt and mix gently. Put aside.

When the rice is almost done, bring about 2 cups water to a boil and add the salted green peas. Cook for about 4–5 minutes. When the rice cooker stops, add drained hot peas and close the lid. Let the rice rest 10–12 minutes before opening lid. With a flat rice paddle, mix gently to fluff up the rice. Serve hot.

© WizData, inc. Shutterstock.

Green Tea Ice Cream

4 servings

- 2 cups (1 pint) good quality vanilla ice cream
- 1 teaspoon powdered green tea (matcha) or to taste
- 1 teaspoon warm water to dilute the green tea powder
- Garnish: 4 pinches green tea powder
- Seasonal fruit if desired

Place the ice cream in a refrigerator for about 30 minutes until it becomes soft enough to mix. In the meantime, dilute the green tea powder with warm water to make a paste. In a mixing bowl, mix the green tea paste into the softened ice cream until the ice cream becomes a beautiful pale green color. Place the bowl in the freezer for about one hour or until the ice cream comes to a consistency that you like.

Serve scoops of ice cream in individual chilled bowls. Garnish each scoop with a sprinkle of green tea powder. Serve with seasonal fruit if desired.

Chef's Note
- When mixing the ice cream with the green tea paste, you may stop sooner for a marbled effect if you wish.

Strange how a teapot can represent at the same time the comforts of solitude and the pleasures of company.

Author unknown

Long after they forget the occasion, they'll remember the setting.

© Elena Kalistratova. Shutterstock.

Africa Adorned

The sights and sounds of my photo safari to Africa will be forever embedded in my mind and in my heart, and memories of that marvelous trip are often shared with family or friends planning a trip to that majestic continent.

My library, where we are surrounded by travel, history, and geography books as well as my African souvenirs and treasured photographs, is the ideal spot to host a reunion dinner with a dear friend whom I met on my trip to Africa.

Exchanging photographs and recalling special memories of Kenya, Tanzania, and Zimbabwe are all part of the evening, which leads to planning another trip together—the next time, a cruise down the Amazon!

Out of Africa Reunion Dinner
Masai Mara Amboseli Celebration
at the home with Jane Goodall

October 10, 2005

Zebra Zombies 6 o'clock
Serengeti Supper 7 o'clock
Photo Exchange 9 o'clock

RSVP 858-666-5555

The Tabletop Landscape

My library desk, set for two intimate friends, is covered by an opulent yellow damask throw, delicately embroidered with lions, tigers, and leopards and edged with silk fringe dripping with golden tassels. The throw sets the mood for this "Out of Africa" evening.

The African theme continues by using leopard chargers on which Lynn Chase Golden Leopard dishes are placed, enhanced by yellow damask napkins held by a fierce leopard napkin ring. Jay Strogwater's exotic animal ornaments are used as place card holders and match the tortoiseshell handles of the flatware.

A leopard-spotted frame under the glow of a lamp announces the evening's agenda, and African books are guarded by an elegantly dressed monkey resting under a bronze palm tree sculpture.

The ambience and memories shared during the evening created a strong desire to return to a land that captured our hearts.

Quick Tips

- Call your local zoo or party animal company and greet your guests with exotic birds on perches, a monkey or a baby elephant, and a keeper dressed in African attire.
- Set up a large tent in your backyard and drape the interior with mosquito netting for that African ambience. Dress your dining table with animal-print fabric—leopard, cheetah, zebra, or giraffe.
- Safari hats for everyone to wear, hung on the back of camp-style dining chair, or bamboo chairs, put everyone in a Masi Mara/Serengeti mood.
- A collection of porcelain, glass, or ceramic animals placed in the middle of your table on mounds of sand, peaking through leafy plants, does the trick at an African-themed party. Buy reptile sand at your local pet store. It is clean, fine, and will make beautiful mounds to hold your animals.
- Visit your travel agent or poster store and purchase maps of Africa. Cover your entire table and use as your tablecloth, or cut the maps into individual placemats.

Menu

- *Chino White Corn Soup*

- *Seared Rare Albacore with Ligurian Black Olive Smashed Potatoes and Shaved Young Artichoke Salad*

- *Lavender Panna Cotta with Chino Strawberry Soup*

GEORGE'S AT THE COVE
1250 Prospect Street
La Jolla, California

Trey Foshee
Executive Chef

Lauded coast to coast, George's at the Cove in La Jolla, California, ranks among Southern California's most popular restaurants. Founder George Hauer is the driving force behind this highly acclaimed restaurant with three levels of spectacular ocean views overlooking the Pacific.

Trey Foshee, formerly executive chef at Robert Redford's Sundance Resort in Utah, is a classically trained graduate of the Culinary Institute of America in Hyde Park, New York. His professional experience includes L'Orangerie in Los Angeles; La Folie in San Francisco; Rockenwagner in Santa Monica; the Sheraton Grand in Los Angeles; and the five-diamond Bay Terrace at the Mauna Lani Bay Hotel and Bungalows in Hawaii.

Named by *Food and Wine* magazine as one of America's ten best chefs in 1998, Trey has received GQ's Golden Dish Award and has appeared in *Bon Appétit, Travel and Leisure,* and *Gourmet* magazines.

Chef Foshee has been guest chef at the prestigious James Beard House in New York, as well as host chef for Hawaii's International Cuisine in the Sun event, with such acclaimed chefs as Charlie Trotter, Emeril Lagasse, and Roger Verge.

Chino White Corn Soup

6 servings

¼ cup butter

¼ cup shallots, sliced

1 cup Noilly Pratt vermouth

4 cups fresh Chino white corn kernels or other white corn

2 cups chicken stock

1 cup half-and-half

½ cup heavy cream

½ teaspoon white pepper, freshly ground

Kosher salt to taste

Heat in 4-quart saucepan over medium heat, melt the butter. Add the shallots and sauté until translucent, approximately 8 minutes. Add the vermouth and reduce until dry. Add the corn and the stock and bring to a simmer and cook 5 minutes. Add the half-and-half and cream and bring back to a simmer. Season with salt and pepper and puree in a blender until smooth. Pass through a fine mesh strainer. The soup can be made to this point in advance and chilled, then reheated when ready to serve.

Chef's Note

- This soup also is great garnished with grilled shrimp, lobster, or smoked salmon or with just a drizzle of crème fraîche and some chives.

- Chino Farms Vegetable Stand
  6123 Calzada Del Bosque
  Rancho Santa Fe, California
  858-756-3184

Seared Rare Albacore with Ligurian Black Olive Smashed Potatoes and Shaved Young Artichoke Salad

4 servings

4 (5-ounce) pieces of albacore

Oil

Salt and pepper

Ligurian Black Olive Smashed Potatoes
  (see recipe that follows)

Shaved Young Artichoke Salad
  (see recipe that follows)

Heat a pan over high heat. Add a little oil. Season the albacore with salt and pepper and sear on all sides, keeping rare on the inside. Slice in one-half inch slices.

Place the potatoes on four plates and top with the sliced albacore. Place the salad on the side.

LIGURIAN BLACK OLIVE SMASHED POTATOES

1 pound Yukon Gold potatoes, peeled

¼ cup Ligurian black olives, pitted and minced

2 tablespoons Italian parsley, chopped

8 tablespoons extra virgin olive oil

Salt and fresh white pepper

In a medium-size pot, add the potatoes and cover with cold water. Season generously with salt and put over medium heat until potatoes are tender. (You can hold them for 45 minutes at this point over low heat.)

When ready to serve, pull the potatoes out with a slotted spoon and place in a mixing bowl. Using a fork, smash the potatoes until there are no large lumps. Add the olives and parsley and the rest of the olive oil. Add a little of the potato cooking liquid, combine well, and season with salt and white pepper to taste.

SHAVED YOUNG ARTICHOKE SALAD

4 young artichokes, fresh

1 lemon, sliced

2 tablespoons lemon juice

3 tablespoons extra virgin olive oil

½ cup arugula sprouts

Salt and white pepper

Break off the outer leaves of the artichokes until you get to the tender inner leaves. Trim off the top of the artichokes. Using a paring knife or vegetable peeler, trim off any green at the base of the artichokes. Rub each artichoke with a sliced lemon to prevent discoloring. Slice the artichokes paper thin into a medium-size bowl. Add the rest of the ingredients and toss to combine.

Lavender Panna Cotta with Chino Strawberry Soup

8 servings

2 cups cream

½ cup + 2 tablespoons milk

1/3 cup granulated sugar

1 fresh vanilla bean, split

4–5 lavender blossoms

half of ¼-ounce packet gelatin

8 (4-ounce) plastic molds

Chino Strawberry Soup
   (see recipe that follows)

Soften the gelatin in cold water. Combine the cream, milk, sugar, lavender, and vanilla bean in a saucepan and bring just to the simmering point and turn off. Remove the gelatin from the water and squeeze out excess water. Add gelatin to the warm cream mixture and stir well to combine. Strain and pour into the molds and chill overnight.

Unmold the panna cotta in a serving bowl. Place some sliced strawberries around and pour the soup around. Garnish with lavender blossoms.

CHINO STRAWBERRY SOUP

½ cup sugar

¾ cup water

2 vanilla beans, split

4 pints Chino strawberries, hulled and rinsed

Combine the sugar, water, and vanilla in a stainless steel pot and bring to a simmer until sugar is completely dissolved; set aside to cool. (This can be made days in advance.) The day before you are going to serve the dessert, slice the strawberries and add to the syrup; let marinate overnight. The next day, place in a blender and puree; then pass through a fine strainer.

Consider your dining room as your theater and your table as your stage and become an award~winning producer and director of your next event.

Style and Supper

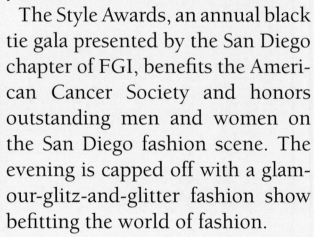

ashion Group International (FGI) is a global nonprofit professional organization established in 1931, with over six thousand members today in the fashion industry and related fields. Designers Donna Karan, Judith Leiber, Diane Von Furstenberg, Pamela Dennis, Dana Buckman, Norma Kamali, and Betsy Johnson are all members of FGI.

The Style Awards, an annual black tie gala presented by the San Diego chapter of FGI, benefits the American Cancer Society and honors outstanding men and women on the San Diego fashion scene. The evening is capped off with a glamour-glitz-and-glitter fashion show befitting the world of fashion.

As a recipient of a Style Award in 2000, it was an honor to host fellow honorees at my home to celebrate their achievements with an evening of delicious cuisine, lively conversation, and entertaining music.

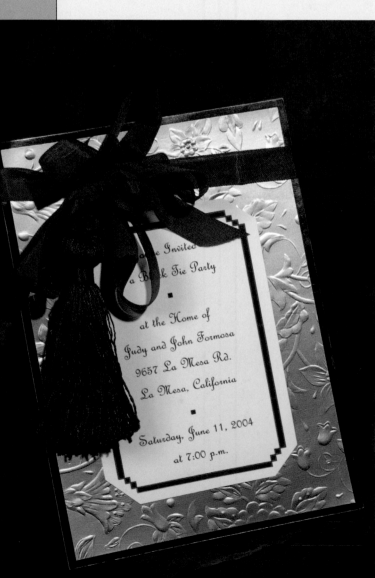

The Tabletop Landscape

French red tulips mixed with leaks, apples, baby artichokes, and garlic fill a black French-inspired gold-footed bowl and is appropriate against the French tapestry titled Le Temps des Cerises.

The elegant E. J. Victor table sets the mood for gold placemats, gold-rimmed chargers and stemware, and gold and white china. Printed satin napkins in shades of yellow celadon and red bring the tapestry colors to the table, and individual Versace-style urns are filled with miniature yellow flowers. The party favors are in silk pouches embellished with small mirrors, reminiscent of the Hall of Mirrors in the Palace of Versaille.

The invitation is placed in the center of the table on an elaborate silver easel, adding another touch of elegance to the table.

This elegant setting is ready to strut the fashion runways of Paris or New York and entertain outstanding honorees in style. Bon appétit!

Quick Tips

- Mixing vegetables (artichokes, asparagus, eggplants) and fruit (apples, lemons, kumquats) in a floral arrangement is a spectacular way to make a centerpiece not only interesting but unique.
- Buy baby artichokes at the grocery store. Cut the stems close to the base of the artichokes, cutting perfectly straight across, so that the artichokes stand up on their own. Wash thoroughly and let dry. Spray with gold spray paint, allow to dry; then tuck a place card in one of the leaves. These elegant artichokes make easy and elegant place card holders!

PATSY BENTIVEGNA

Private Executive Chef / Cooking Instructor
Ponte Vedra Beach, Florida
ChefPatsy@hotmail.com

Private chef Patsy Bentivegna, a native Californian, began her culinary career in her family's kitchen, baking and cooking for her parents and five siblings.

Over the last twenty-five years, Patsy has used her natural talent and her love of cooking to create a successful culinary career as a caterer, café chef, wholesale bakery owner, and pastry chef. You may have had the pleasure of experiencing her culinary expertise at some of San Diego's most successful establishments, including Top of the Market, Rancho Valencia Resort, and Pamplemousse Grill, as well as her own establishments Morning Glory Café and Girlfriends Baking Co.

Patsy was winner of the KPBS Chocolate Lovers Contest and has appeared on NBC News and the CBS Morning Show. Her award-winning recipes and outstanding reviews in prominent newspapers and magazines make her everyone's favorite chef.

One of Patsy's most memorable experiences was working as pastry chef for San Francisco's Bradley Ogden, executive chef and owner of One Market and Lark Creek Inn, during one of his consulting contracts with Rancho Valencia Resort. Chef Bentivegna says it was from him that she gained a true appreciation for what it takes to achieve flavor without compromising the integrity of the ingredients.

Ponte Vedra Beach, Florida, is now her home where she is affectionately known as "Chef Patsy" to her clients and students. Her passion for the culinary arts and a desire to share "her food" has expanded her client based to New York, Chicago and even a barbeque competition in Des Moines, Iowa. A cooking show is in the works, so stay tuned. You may see Chef Patsy on your local television network in the very near future.

Menu

- ❧ *Martini Cantaloupe Ceviche*

- ❧ *Strawberry Fields Salad*

- ❧ *Pork Tenderloin Wellington with Apple and Apricot Goat Cheese Filling*

- ❧ *Herb-Roasted New Potatoes*

- ❧ *Spring Green Beans with Fresh Basil and Zest of Lemon*

- ❧ *White Chocolate Lime Mousse Tart with Fresh Blueberries*

Martini Cantaloupe Ceviche

8 servings, martini-glass size

A swanky presentation of a refreshing and light appetizer to begin any elegant dinner.

>2 cantaloupes
>½ pound prosciutto, thinly sliced and chopped into small pieces
>1 medium red onion, finely minced
>2 English cucumbers, peeled, seeded, and diced
>4 heads Belgian endives
>½ cup fresh lime juice and zest of 1 lime
>½ cup fresh orange juice and zest of 1 orange
>¼ cup finely chopped fresh basil
>½ cup olive oil
>½ teaspoon salt
>¼ teaspoon pepper
>*Garnish:* 8 small basil leaves

Reserve 8 endive leaves for garnish and cut endive into 2-inch matchsticks. Refrigerate until ready to serve.

Cut melons in half. Scoop out seeds. Using a melon scoop, cut small balls from each melon and place in a large mixing bowl. Add remaining ingredients; toss and refrigerate until ready to serve.

Evenly divide endive matchsticks into each martini glass. Fill glass with ceviche mixture and garnish with reserved endive and basil leaves and serve.

Strawberry Fields Salad

6 servings

Always a springtime favorite, this is an elegant salad that combines the sweetness of strawberries with the pungent buttery flavor of gorgonzola cheese and the crunchy flavor of caramelized walnuts. The vinaigrette is light, with the crisp, clean flavor of the rice vinegar.

>1 pound mixed field greens, clean and dry
>1 pint fresh strawberries, sliced
>4 ounces Gorgonzola cheese, crumbled
>1 cup walnuts, whole
>1 tablespoon butter, unsalted
>2 teaspoons granulated sugar
>3 tablespoons extra virgin olive oil
>1 tablespoon rice vinegar, chilled
>Salt and pepper

Melt butter in a small skillet and sauté whole walnuts on medium heat for 1 minute. Sprinkle sugar over walnuts and continue to sauté until the walnuts are caramelized and golden. Remove from pan; cool. After walnuts have cooled, chop coarse, leaving a few whole for garnish. Set aside until ready to serve.

Mix olive oil and rice vinegar in a bottle and shake well.

Place greens, strawberries, and cheese in large mixing bowl. Drizzle vinaigrette over salad ingredients and lightly toss. Add salt and pepper to taste. Sprinkle chopped nuts over top. Add the reserved whole walnuts as a garnish and serve.

Pork Tenderloin Wellington with Apple and Apricot Goat Cheese Filling

6 servings

This is an elegant main course, perfect for a special dinner. The filling of sautéed apples, dried apricots, and shallots is enhanced by a white wine reduction. The addition of goat cheese not only binds the ingredients together but adds a savory flavor, further enhanced by fresh thyme. The true elegance of this dish is displayed by the rich and flaky puff pastry that can be decorated to accommodate any festive dinner.

- 2 pork tenderloins (approximately 1½ pounds each, trimmed to 8 inches long and 3 inches wide)
- 2 puff pastry sheets, thawed (1 for each tenderloin)
- 1 tablespoon olive oil
- 1 egg, beaten
- Salt and pepper
- Apple and Apricot Goat Cheese Filling (*see recipe that follows*)
- 2 additional puff pastry sheets, thawed, to be used to decorate the Wellington, if desired.

Heat a large sauté pan to medium high. Add oil and sear pork tenderloins for 3 minutes on each side. Salt and pepper; then set aside until ready to assemble Wellington.

Preheat oven to 400°. Line a baking sheet with parchment paper. Roll out defrosted puff pastry sheet on a lightly floured surface to fit the dimensions of the tenderloin. Brush the edges with the beaten egg and set the tenderloin in the center of the pastry sheet.

Pack half the filling on the tenderloin. Lift one side of the pastry sheet and cover top of filling and the tenderloin. Continue to gently roll the tenderloin in a jellyroll style to completely cover the tenderloin, placing the seam on the bottom to create a smooth pastry top. Fold the pastry ends under the rolled tenderloin and press to secure the pastry to create a neat package. Brush pastry with beaten egg. Repeat process for second tenderloin.

From extra pastry, cut out desired shapes (leaves, fruits, Easter shapes, etc.) and decorate the top of the Wellington, brushing added pastry shapes with beaten egg.

Place in 400° oven and bake until pastry has puffed and is a beautiful golden brown, approximately 30 minutes. Remove from oven and rest for a few minutes before serving.

APPLE AND APRICOT GOAT CHEESE FILLING

- ½ cup goat cheese (4 ounces)
- 1 tablespoon olive oil
- 1 tablespoon butter, unsalted
- 1 tablespoon fresh thyme, minced
- 2 tablespoons shallots, minced
- 2 large Granny Smith apples, peeled and sliced
- 1 cup dried apricots, coarsely chopped
- ½ cup white wine

Heat a large sauté pan on medium high; add oil and butter. Then add shallots and sauté until soft and translucent. Add fruit and continue to sauté until apples are slightly softened but still firm. Deglaze the fruit with the wine and add the salt, pepper, and thyme.

Lower the heat and simmer the filling mixture until the liquid has almost dissolved. The apples should hold their shape and not have the appearance of applesauce.

Remove pan from the heat and transfer mixture to a mixing bowl. Fold the goat cheese into the hot mixture. Cool filling and set aside until ready to assemble Wellington.

Herb-Roasted New Potatoes

6 servings

2 pounds small red potatoes, washed, quartered, and dried

1 tablespoon fresh thyme leaves, whole

1 tablespoon fresh rosemary, chopped

1 tablespoon olive oil

Salt and pepper

Preheat oven to 400°. Place potatoes onto a large baking sheet. Drizzle oil over potatoes and toss. Sprinkle herbs on top of potatoes and continue to toss. Add salt and pepper. Place in oven and bake. Roast until golden brown and the potatoes are tender, approximately 30–40 minutes. Remove from oven and serve.

Spring Green Beans with Fresh Basil and Zest of Lemon

6 servings

1 pound fresh green beans, washed and trimmed

1 teaspoon lemon zest

1 tablespoon fresh basil, chopped

1 teaspoon olive oil

1 teaspoon butter, unsalted

Salt and pepper

In a large saucepan of salted boiling water, cook beans approximately 1 minute, until crisp. (Beans should be bright green in color.) Drain the blanched beans and immediately place in a large bowl of ice water to stop the cooking process and cool. After beans have cooled, drain and set aside.

Melt butter in a large skillet and add oil. When pan is at a medium heat, lightly sauté the blanched green beans until they are completely heated. Add lemon zest, basil, and salt and pepper to taste. Remove from pan and serve.

White Chocolate Lime Mousse Tart with Fresh Blueberries

8 servings

This show-stopping dessert is a must for any special occasion. The combination of white chocolate and the tart citrus flavor of fresh lime creates a rich and creamy dessert.

4 ounces butter, unsalted (very cold and cut into small pieces)

1 tablespoon sugar

¼ teaspoon kosher salt

1¼ cups all-purpose unbleached flour

¼ cup heavy whipping cream

White Chocolate Lime Mousse Filling *(see recipe that follows)*

Garnish: fresh blueberries; lime zest

Preheat oven 350°. Add dry ingredients to food processor bowl and pulse a few times until ingredients are blended. Add butter and pulse until mixture resembles coarse meal (small peas). Do not overmix. Add cream and mix until the dough pulls from the side of the bowl and forms a ball. Form dough into a disk shape, wrap in plastic and chill for 30 minutes. (Dough can be frozen at this point for future use.)

Roll out dough to a 12-inch circle. Place dough into 9-inch tart pan and press around the edges to form a nice crust. Line the inside of the dough with heavy aluminum foil and gently form the foil over the edges of the tart shell. Pierce holes with a fork through the foil to prevent shrinkage and chill for at least 20 minutes before baking. Bake for 35–40 minutes until golden brown. Remove from oven and cool.

Spread filling evenly in cooled tart shell. Chill for at least 4 hours before serving. When filling is firm, remove tart from pan and place on serving plate. Using reserved whipping cream (from filling recipe), decorate tart; top with fresh blueberries and lime zest. Refrigerate until ready to serve.

Chef's Note

- For best results, mix the tart shell in a food processor.

White Chocolate Lime Mousse Filling

2 eggs

½ cup sugar

¼ cup fresh lime juice

4 ounces white chocolate

1½ cups heavy whipping cream

1 cup fresh blueberries

1 tablespoon fresh lime zest

Whisk sugar, lime juice, and eggs in the top of a double boiler. Cook until mixture is thick enough to coat the back of a spoon. Do not boil. Remove from heat, add white chocolate, and mix until completely blended; then cool.

Using an electric mixer, whip cream until peaks are firm. Reserve one-third of whipped cream and chill until needed (for decorating top of tart). Gently fold remaining whipped cream into cooled lime mixture.

Sit your guests down to a beautiful table and get up from your meal to a standing ovation!

Tropical Nights in Paradise

Steven Bernstein, ASID, an innovative and inspired interior designer and an avid car enthusiast, is happiest when he entertains his friends from the Jaguar and Thunderbird car clubs he belongs to. His invitations regularly summon "Big Cats" (the Jaguar Club) and Little Birds (the Thunderbird Club) to his home to celebrate their mutual passion for cars.

His eclectic home is regularly on display for interior design fundraising tours, and his collections of china, crystal, and antique linens are regularly brought out for dinner parties.

His U-shaped home inspired me to create a tropical table next to his inviting pool, giant ferns, and imposing palm trees, where Big Cat and Little Bird friends enjoy warm summer breezes, cool tropical drinks, and spicy Thai cuisine.

Steven is a gracious host, and all of us could learn from his enthusiasm for life, entertaining, and the love of friends.

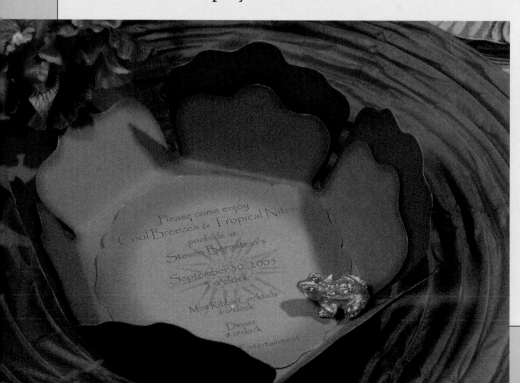

Please come enjoy
Cool Breezes & Tropical Nites
poolside at
Steven Bernstein's
September 30, 2005
5 o'clock
Mint Ribbon Cocktails
6 o'clock
Dinner
8 o'clock
Entertainment

The Tabletop Landscape

A lazy silk frog is the guest of honor on this tropical tablescape and rests happily on a lily pad surrounded by orchids and exotic plants.

A brown and green striped runner down the middle of the square table creates a path for the frog to follow and lies on top of a giant-banana-leaf tablecloth. Rattan chargers hold fluid lime green, open-petal china, continuing the tropical theme.

Enamel green frog napkin rings hold cream-colored napkins edged in two tones of green, and a trumpet flower tucked in the folds of the napkins holds the name of each guest. A small porcelain frog holds a mini vase filled with an orchid for each guest to take home as a remembrance of the evening.

Green stemware and bamboo-handled flatware complete the tropical tablescape, and the patio chairs are decorated with giant lily pads, completing the tropical ambience.

Quick Tips

- Use fruit such as cantaloupe, melons, apples, oranges, or pineapples as containers for exotic florals. Make the fruit part of the arrangement. With a very sharp knife and a melon scooper, dig out a hole big enough to hold a small vase or floral tube, depending on the size of the fruit. Put flowers into the vase or floral tube and position in the fruit.

- Take advantage of the beautiful color of fruit. Cut fruit such as a watermelon in half and then in half again, so that you have four large pieces. Place in a rustic wood container and set the container on banana leaves or giant palm leaves. Surround the container with tropical-looking flowers such as Tiger Lilies, and tuck some of the flowers right into the watermelon.

- Cover your patio table with giant banana leaves, which will serve as your tablecloth. On smaller leaves from your garden, (lemon leaves) write guests' names with a gold ink pen and use the leaves as your place cards.

ROY'S LA JOLLA

Costa Verde Shopping Center
8760 Genesee Avenue
San Diego, California

Evan Cruz
Executive Chef and Partner

Evan Cruz, an aspiring young chef, was born in the Philippines and raised in San Diego, California. He recalls taking an interest in cooking from a very young age and learning to cook from his grandmother, who always encouraged him. He discovered his calling in the culinary arts at age fifteen while working for a Marriott hotel during summer vacation.

While studying at the California Culinary Academy in San Francisco, Evan met the father of Hawaiian fusion cuisine, Roy Yamaguchi, and in 2002, after paying his dues in a variety of positions, Evan was offered an opportunity to replace one of his mentors, David Abella, as executive chef at Roy's La Jolla.

Since then, Roy's La Jolla has been awarded "Best Ethnic Restaurant 2003" by the California Restaurant Association, and Chef Cruz was named "Chef Partner of the Year" for Roy's restaurants.

Menu

   ❧ *Pan-Seared Black Cod with Lotus Leaf Rice*

   ❧ *Asian-Style Black Bean Soup*

   ❧ *Char Sui Shrimp and Glass Noodle Salad with Lemongrass Ginger Vinaigrette*

   ❧ *Hoisin-Braised Chinatown Duck with Lup Cheong Fried Rice*

   ❧ *Korean Barbecue Kobe Beef with Mung Bean Pancakes and Koo Ju Jang Butter*

Pan-Seared Black Cod with Lotus Leaf Rice

4 servings

4 (3-ounce) pieces black cod

Canola oil

Seasonings

Lotus Leaf Rice (*see recipe that follows*)

When rice is nearly done, heat sauté pan coated lightly with canola oil. Season cod and sear on both sides until desired doneness is reached. Place rice in the middle of the plate and arrange fish on top.

LOTUS LEAF RICE

4 dried lotus leaves, soaked in water overnight

1 cup mochi rice (Japanese sticky rice)

1½ cups water

4 tablespoons sesame oil

10 sliced shiitake mushrooms, medium sliced

4 tablespoons oyster sauce

2 tablespoons dried shrimp

4 tablespoons diced white onion

1 tablespoon ginger, small diced

1 tablespoon garlic, small diced

1 small lup cheong sausage (optional), diced

Wash rice thoroughly under cold water until running water becomes clear. In a hot sauté pan, add sesame oil and sauté off shiitake mushrooms and onion. Add garlic, ginger, sausage, and shrimp. Add rice and sauté until rice is light brown. Rice might start to stick together and form; this is OK.

Line a 2-inch bamboo steamer with 1 lotus leaf. Place the rice mixture in the middle, spread out evenly, and add the water. Make sure none of the rice is above the water. Place another lotus leaf on top of rice and steam for 25 minutes.

Take out of steamer and let cool. Take the other 2 lotus leaves and divide them in quarters. Take 1 cup cooked rice and place in one-quarter leaf; fold leaf over rice until it becomes a bundle. Take another quarter leaf and make 2 1-inch strips the length of the leaf; then take the rest of the leaf and wrap the bundle again crosswise. Use the 2 strips as twine to wrap and secure the bundle. Repeat to create 4 bundles. Steam the bundles for another 10 minutes.

Asian-Style Black Bean Soup

4–6 servings

1 cup olive oil

4 ounces pancetta, small diced

2 cups diced white or yellow onion

3 large shallots

1 tablespoon sautéed shrimp paste

1 tablespoon minced garlic

1 tablespoon green curry paste

2 tablespoons minced ginger

1 stalk lemongrass, rough chopped

1 teaspoon ground cumin

1 pound black turtle beans, cleaned and soaked overnight

3 quarts lobster stock

3 kaffir lime leaves

1 bunch Thai basil, picked

Salt to taste

Freshly ground black pepper to taste

1 red bell pepper, finely diced

1 yellow bell pepper, finely diced

Fresh lime juice to taste

Garnish: fresh cilantro sprigs

Heat oil in a heavy-bottomed pan. Sauté pancetta until rendered. Remove excess fat. Add onions, garlic, and ginger and sauté until soft and lightly caramelized. Add green curry paste and sauté until fragrant. Add shrimp paste; sauté. Add beans (drained), stock, lemongrass, lime leaves, Thai basil, and 2 quarts of lobster stock.

Bring to a boil; then simmer gently until beans are tender (do not season with salt or pepper until after the beans are cooked). After 45 minutes' cooking time, stir in bell peppers. Puree half of the soup and combine with the remaining soup. Add remaining parsley, lime juice, lemon zest, and sugar to taste. Season with salt and pepper and adjust consistency with additional stock (or water) as needed.

Pour soup into 6 warmed soup bowls. Serve garnished with fresh cilantro sprigs.

Char Sui Shrimp and Glass Noodle Salad with Lemongrass Ginger Vinaigrette

4 servings

½ package char sui mix powder

3 tablespoons sake

12 extra jumbo shrimp, peeled and deveined

6 tablespoons hoisin sauce

2 tablespoons sambal paste

2 tablespoons ginger

½ tablespoon garlic

2 tablespoons soy sauce

1 package mung bean thread noodles (glass noodles)

2 baby bok choy, blanched, julienne

¼ head red cabbage, julienne

2 carrots, julienne

1 red bell pepper, julienne

1 green bell pepper, julienne

1 yellow bell pepper, julienne

¼ cup mung beans

Nam Plah Vinaigrette
   (see recipe that follows)

Lemongrass Ginger Vinaigrette
   (see recipe that follows)

8 leaves green leaf lettuce (such as baby romaine or Lolla Rosa)

Garnish: popcorn sprouts and kaiware sprouts (daikon sprouts), optional

In a small bowl, mix hoisin sauce, garlic, ginger, soy sauce, and sambal paste. In a separate bowl, rehydrate powdered char sui mix with sake and add to mixture. Marinate shrimp for 2 hours.

Grill shrimp on medium heat. Be careful not to burn the tails.

Place greens on bottom of the plate; mix the glass noodles and vegetables and arrange in middle of the greens. Dress glass noodle mix with Lemongrass Ginger Vinaigrette. Lightly dress shrimp with Nam Plah Vinaigrette before placing over salad. Arrange shrimp on, around, or atop the mixture. Garnish with popcorn sprouts and kaiware sprouts if desired.

LEMONGRASS GINGER VINAIGRETTE

1 tablespoon spicy sesame oil (rayu)

3 tablespoons lemongrass, minced

1 tablespoon kaffir lime leaf, minced

1 tablespoon garlic, minced

2 tablespoons ginger, minced

3 tablespoons shallots, minced

2 tablespoons fish sauce

¾ cup lime juice

¼ cup rice wine vinegar

2 tablespoons chili sauce (siriacha)

2 tablespoons brown sugar

¾ cup peanut oil

½ cup blended oil

1 tablespoon minced cilantro

1 tablespoon minced mint

1 tablespoon minced Thai basil

Heat sesame oil in a sauté pan over medium-low heat. Add lemongrass, lime leaf, garlic, ginger, and shallots. Sauté until softened (do not allow to brown). Add fish sauce, lime juice, vinegar, chili sauce, and brown sugar. Reduce by one-fourth and remove from heat. Allow to cool. Using a wire whisk, gradually incorporate peanut and blended oil in a thin steady stream. Add herbs and mix well.

NAM PLAH VINAIGRETTE

1 lemon, juiced

2 limes, juiced

3 oranges, juiced

6 tablespoons sweet chili sauce

1 tablespoon fish sauce

2 tablespoons sambal

¼ bunch mint; leaves only, chiffonade

¼ bunch cilantro; leaves only, chiffonade

2 each shallots, shaved

4 cloves garlic, shaved

2 teaspoons crushed red pepper flakes

Whisk thoroughly in a mixing bowl to combine.

Chef's Note

The products available at 99 Ranch Market, 7330 Clairemont Mesa Blvd., San Diego, CA 92111, phone (858) 565-7799; and also at Mitsuwa Market, 4240 Kearny Mesa Rd., San Diego, CA 92111, phone (858) 569-6699.

Hoisin-Braised Chinatown Duck with Lup Cheong Fried Rice

4 servings

1 whole duck

1 bunch cilantro, washed

1 bunch scallions, washed

1½ cups young Hawaiian ginger, pounded

1 whole garlic, crushed

2 cups hoisin sauce

2 stalks lemongrass (rough chop)

1 small handful kaffir limes

1 cup honey

2 star anise pods

2 cups plum sauce

1 gallon chicken stock

Garnish: julienne scallions; plucked cilantro

1 yard butcher's twine

Lup Cheong Fried Rice
    (*see recipe that follows*)

In a large pot, mix hoisin, 1½ cups plum sauce, honey, ginger, garlic, ½ bunch cilantro, chicken stock, lemongrass, scallions, and star anise pods; bring to a boil. Turn down to a simmer.

Clean out duck and wash out inner cavity. Cut off and remove any excess fat from the carcass. Push down both thighs and crack the thigh joint to release the leg bone. Turn the duck so that the breast is breast side up and closest to you. Take wing tips and tuck behind the drumette, so that it forms a triangle. Run twine underneath the hips of the duck so that there is an equal amount of twine on each side.

Take ends of twine and cross where ends of legs cross, cross again underneath to have end points under the thigh portions. Flip duck over (having breast side down) and run each point noosed around the neck portion of duck, making sure that the wings are also tucked under the twine. Tighten the twine so that the twine has no excess slack.

Place duck in liquid, breast side down first. Turn duck over every half hour. Cook for about 1½ hours.

Take duck out of liquid and let rest, breast side up for about half an hour. Fine chop cilantro and add to the rest of the plum sauce. Evenly glaze the duck, and finish in the 350° oven for about 15 minutes or until duck looks glossy.

Serve duck sliced atop a mound of fried rice. Garnish with cilantro sprigs.

LUP CHEONG FRIED RICE

2 cups jasmine rice (day old, or cold)

3 lup cheong sausages, small diced

1 bunch cilantro, fine chopped

5 shallots, small diced

1 yellow bell pepper, fine diced

1 red bell pepper, fine diced

1 green bell pepper, fine diced

2 tablespoons garlic, minced

2 tablespoons ginger, minced

1 tablespoon curry powder

4 tablespoons sesame oil

2 tablespoons peanut oil

2 tablespoons oyster sauce

Soy sauce to taste

In a hot sauté pan, add peanut oil and lup cheong sausage, stir fry. Add shallots, bell peppers and garlic and ginger, stir fry. Add sesame oil and rice. Lightly stir fry until rice starts to pop and sizzle. Add oyster sauce and soy sauce to taste.

Korean Barbecue Kobe Beef with Mung Bean Pancakes and Koo Ju Jang Butter

4 servings

1½ pounds Kobe beef (can use prime rib eye steak or New York steak)

1 cup soy sauce

1 cup sugar

½ cup brown or palm sugar

½ cup koo ju jang paste

½ cup ginger, minced

½ cup garlic, minced

1 bunch scallions, chopped

2½ cups white sesame seeds

¼ cup chili flakes

¼ cup spicy sesame oil (rayu)

Mung Bean Pancakes
    (*see recipe that follows*)

Koo Ju Jang Butter (*see recipe that follows*)

In a large bowl, mix soy sauce and both sugars until all the sugar dissolves. Add koo ju jang paste and mix until well incorporated. Add ginger, garlic, and scallions. In a medium sauté pan, add white sesame seeds; sauté until lightly toasted and fragrant. Remove from heat; add chili flakes and sauté. Add sesame oil. Pour sesame oil mixture into large bowl with other ingredients and blend. Cover beef with marinade and refrigerate for 4 hours.

Cook beef to desired temperature; let rest and slice thinly. Place three pancakes on bottom of each plate, evenly distribute the beef in the middle of the pancakes, and garnish with Koo Ju Jang Butter and white sesame seeds.

MUNG BEAN PANCAKES

1 cup mung beans

1 cup pancake flour

1 cup mochiko flour

½ cup scallions, chopped (green part only)

¼ cup Japanese 7-spice (Shichimi togarashi)

Fish sauce to taste

Shrimp paste to taste

Ice water (quantity will vary)

1 egg white

Mix all dry ingredients in a large bowl. Slowly incorporate water and egg white, using only enough water to form a thin pancake-batter consistency. Add scallions and mung beans. Season with the 7-spice, fish sauce, and shrimp paste to taste. Batter should have some lumps. Test batter by making one pancake; it will rise very slightly. Using a 1-ounce ladle, make 12–14 pancakes; keep in a warm place until ready to serve.

KOO JU JANG BUTTER

2 tablespoons sesame oil

1 teaspoon chopped garlic

1 tablespoon chopped ginger

1 cup mung beans

2 stalks green onions

1 tablespoon white sesame seeds

4 tablespoons sesame seeds (for garnish)

In a warm sauté pan, add 1 ounce sesame oil, garlic, ginger, scallions, and mung beans, stir-fry briefly and set aside.

Dining by Design is what elevates ordinary life into a celebration!

Seaside Soiree

The Laguna Design Center, in conjunction with the Philharmonic Society of Orange County, invites designers, showrooms, and interior design students to participate in "Entertaining by Design," an annual fund-raiser of tabletop designs that invites everyone to experience the fascinating world of interior design and entertaining. Designers demonstrate their talent and expertise for a great cause during the annual two-day event.

Spectacular tabletop displays created by some of Southern California's top designers are the premier attraction at the popular open house. Blake House Associates, Inc., one of the most elegant showrooms at the center, asked Debby Neville—owner of Total Image and instructor at the Interior Designers Institute in Newport Beach, Dru White interior designer, and graduate of the Institute—to assist students in creating a tabletop design on Peter Alexander's magnificent dining room table.

Owner Sandy MacLennon and general manager Stephen Anderson were delighted with the tabletop design by Kathleen Bouvier, Bonnie Flamm, Davana Greenamyer, Pat Cavaretta, and Krysti Todd Gutherie. These future designers promise to be among the best designers in the country, as you will see for yourself.

Shrimp and Crab Chowder

8 servings

 2 tablespoons olive oil

 4 stalks green onion, diced

 3 cloves garlic, chopped

 1 (18-ounce) can chopped tomatoes, with juice

 1 cup dry white wine

 Salt and pepper

 3 cups water

 2 cups diced white potatoes

 4 clusters Snow crab or Dungeness crab

 1 pound small shrimp

 Garnish: 4 tablespoons chopped cilantro

 Wonton Garnish (*see recipe that follows*)

Heat the olive oil in a saucepan or Dutch oven over medium heat. Add green onion and garlic; cook 2 minutes. Add tomatoes, white wine, salt and pepper, water, and crab sections. Cook on low, covered, for approximately 15 minutes.

Remove the crab clusters and cool. Remove crab from shell and return to the pot. Add white potatoes and shrimp and cook until potatoes are 90 percent done; remove from heat. Adjust the water level, and if crab does not produce a dominating taste, add a little lobster or crab base.

Place soup in bowl and top with Wonton Garnish and sprinkle with chopped cilantro.

WONTON GARNISH

 1 large clove garlic, roasted

 2 (6 x 6) wonton skins

 4 tablespoons gorgonzola cheese

Heat oven to 375°. Cut top off garlic bulb and drizzle with olive oil. Place in the oven, covered, for approximately 20 minutes or until garlic becomes soft and caramelized. Remove from oven and cool. Cut wonton skins into quarters. Spread with a little roasted garlic and top with gorgonzola cheese and place in the oven until cheese is melted and wonton is crispy.

Warm Sesame Goat Cheese Salad

6 servings

 16 ounces baby field greens

 1 pint fresh raspberries

 1 pint yellow pear tomatoes

 ½ loaf brioche bread

 ½ cup pine nuts, toasted

 1 cup goat cheese, crumbled

 4 tablespoons black sesame seeds

 4 tablespoons white sesame seeds

 10 ounces Maple Balsamic Dressing (*see recipe that follows*)

 Garnish: chopped chives

Wash all greens, cover with a damp paper towel and place in the refrigerator. Cut goat cheese in medallions and rest in the mixture of black and white sesame seeds; coat thoroughly and place in the refrigerator.

Heat oven to 375°. Cut brioche into triangles, drizzle with a little olive oil and salt and pepper, and place in the oven until crisp. Remove and leave at room temperature.

Place greens on a plate. Arrange 4 berries and 4 tomatoes per plate in an even pattern around greens, alternating berry, tomato, berry, tomato. Place brioche off to one side of the salad, sprinkle the salad with toasted pine nuts. Place goat cheese in the oven until it becomes soft; place on the top of the salad and drizzle with dressing. Garnish with finely chopped chives.

MAPLE BALSAMIC DRESSING

1 cup olive oil

3 tablespoons aged balsamic vinegar

2 tablespoons maple syrup

Salt and pepper

Place oil, vinegar, and maple syrup in a bowl, season with salt and pepper, and mix.

Cedar Plank-Roasted Halibut over Fingerling and Peruvian Potatoes with Arugula and Roasted Vegetables

4 servings

4 cedar planks, approximately 12 inches long

4 (7-ounce) portions halibut filet, deboned

5 fingerling potatoes, quartered and cut lengthwise

6 Peruvian potatoes, quartered and cut lengthwise

2 cups arugula

32 asparagus spears

16 baby carrots

16 baby zucchini

Salt, pepper, and garlic to taste

Lemon Chive Oil (*see recipe that follows*)

9 ounces Warm Tomato and Shiitake Vinaigrette (*see recipe that follows*)

Garnish: chives, finely diced and strands

Cut halibut filets into proper portions, rub with olive oil and salt and pepper. Cover and place in refrigerator. Place potatoes in bowl and coat with olive oil, salt and pepper, and garlic. Cover and place in refrigerator.

Blanch asparagus in hot water; remove and place in ice bath until chilled. Cover and place in refrigerator. Coat remaining vegetables with olive oil and salt and pepper and place in refrigerator.

Soak cedar planks in water for over 1 hour. Place potatoes and vegetables on a cookie sheet. Place in a 375° oven until cooked. Remove and set out. Place cedar planks in the oven for 10 minutes. Remove and place the fish on planks. Return to the oven and, depending on thickness, cook 10 minutes or until interior flesh is cooked through (not transparent). When fish is close to done, place vegetables and potatoes in the oven to heat; also heat a sauté pan to high, drizzle with olive oil, and place arugula in pan. Sprinkle with salt and pepper and flash sauté to 50 percent done.

When ready to serve, remove all ingredients and set up plates. Place asparagus in a square in the center of the plate, with stalks overlapping each other. Place potatoes in the square and arrange other vegetables half in the center of asparagus and half outside asparagus. Place arugula over potatoes and place the fish on top of all ingredients. Drizzle fish with oil and drizzle around the plate with heated vinaigrette. Garnish with a small amount of chopped chives on top and two strands of whole chive.

LEMON CHIVE OIL

1 cup olive oil

6 chives

Zest of 1 lemon

Salt and pepper

In a blender or food processor, emulsify until ingredients are blended; strain through cheesecloth or strainer.

WARM TOMATO SHIITAKE VINAIGRETTE

5 tomatoes, cooked, seeded, and skinned

1 teaspoon chopped garlic

½ cup shiitake mushrooms

Salt and pepper

5 tablespoons rice vinegar

2 tablespoons olive oil

Sauté mushrooms in olive oil until soft. Place all ingredients in a blender and blend until smooth. Remove and strain. Transfer to a saucepan to heat.

Individual Spoon-Served Crème Brulee with Fresh Berry Compote and Citrus Whipped Cream

1¼ quarts (5 cups) heavy cream

½ vanilla bean, split

1 cup sugar

10 egg yolks, beaten

Fresh Berry Compote
   (*see recipe that follows*)

Citrus Whipped Cream
   (*see recipe that follows*)

Garnish: fresh mint sprigs

Combine heavy cream, vanilla bean, and half the sugar. Bring to a boil. Combine the egg yolks and remaining sugar. Temper egg-sugar mixture into hot heavy cream; cook until thick enough to coat the back of a spoon; strain through a fine sieve. Fill Asian soup spoons with mixture 1/8 full and place into an ice bath.

Bake at 325° approximately 20 minutes or until set. Remove from water and cool. Refrigerate overnight. When ready to serve, coat each spoon with a light dusting of sugar, and burn sugar with a butane torch.

Place a tablespoon of berry compote in the center of a plate, top with a generous portion of whipped cream. Place 4 spoons of crème brulee evenly around the berries in the center and garnish with sprigs of fresh mint.

FRESH BERRY COMPOTE

2 pints raspberries

1 pint blueberries

1 pint strawberries

3 tablespoons white wine

2 tablespoons sugar

In a saucepan combine fruit, wine, and sugar. Cook on low until fruit begins to cook through; gently stir. When juices begin to thicken, remove from the heat and chill.

CITRUS WHIPPED CREAM

½ quart heavy cream

Juice of 1 orange

Juice of 1 lemon

Juice of 1 lime

4 tablespoons sugar

Combine all ingredients in a mixing bowl
and whip until cream becomes stiff; store
in the refrigerator.

*People eat
with their eyes!*

*Table design and cuisine must marry well
for your guests to have the maximum experience!*

Elegant Mozart Gala

A table draped with exquisite linens and set with elegant china and crystal is a feast for the eyes and a lift for the soul.

The Prodigy and His Piano

The birth of Wolfgang Amadeus Mozart in 1756 in Salsburg, Austria, is cause for celebration around the world. In San Diego, California, Mozart's birthday is celebrated at a yearly fund-raising gala that includes delicious cuisine, exquisite wine, elegant and creative tables, and glorious Mozart music.

Guests dressed in their finest sweep into the ballroom and marvel at each table decorated by individual interior designers, artists, floral shops, as well as design teams from major department stores, including Neiman Marcus, Tiffany & Co., Nordstrom, and Saks Fifth Avenue.

After viewing what has been dubbed the "Rose Parade of Tabletops," patrons find their table, enjoy their gourmet meal, and take pleasure after dessert in a Mozart concert conducted by Maestro David Atherton.

It has been my pleasure to participate in this marvelous event year after year. Designing exciting tabletops for the Mainly Mozart Gala is great fun but also a challenge. Every year I must create a tabletop different from the previous year, while also keeping in mind the tabletops designed by thirty other very talented designers.

The first table I am presenting to you is a very elegantly dressed traditional table that I named "The Prodigy and His Piano."

The Tabletop Landscape

A striped silk taffeta table skirt in shades of rose, yellow, and two tones of celadon is overlaid with a custom table-cloth in a print fabric of antique roses and pale yellow butterflies, edged with pink and green tassels and fringe

A small piano sits as the center of attention with antique hand-painted instruments and sheet music. The open piano top reveals a cascade of blush pink and white roses.

The crystal and gold-rimmed chargers are embellished with a gold M monogram to remind guests that they are at Mozart's table. Royal Doulton's Litchfield china and the delicate flatware, Yamazaki's Victoria Gold, add an elegant touch and match the crystal stemware.

The napkin holder is an elegant silver-footed antique ring that holds a bud vase with a fragrant rose. Votives encrusted with pearls and faux diamonds sit like jewels around the foot of the piano and enhance the menu card in a pearl and silver frame.

The place card, a miniature music book, sits on a silver piano filled with chocolate violins, which guests delight in taking home.

Quick Tips

- Inexpensive votives can be embellished by gluing pearls and faux jewels to match the décor.
- Buy gold or silver stick-on initials (used for the back of envelopes) to give your chargers a personalized look.
- Plain chargers can be embellished with faux gems around the far edges for an elegant look. Rhinestones or pearls add that rich, elegant look. Buy packages of faux jewels at your local craft store. (one side should be flat) Decide on how you want to place them around the edge of your charger, use white tacky glue to adhere to your charger.

A great way to personalize your charger and coordinate with the theme of your table.

LE FONTAINEBLEAU

The Westgate Hotel
1055 Second Avenue
San Diego, California

Fabrice Hardel
Executive Chef

Originally from Normandy, France, executive chef Fabrice Hardel brings sixteen years' experience spanning two continents to the Westgate Hotel. His career began in France, where he served as a commis chef at several prestigious restaurants, including La Chaine d'Or Hotel, rated with one Michelin star and fifteen points by Gault Millau.

Fabrice honed his culinary skills as chef de partie at the Hotel Luxembourg; Le Lion d'Or Hotel in France; Brockencote Hall Hotel (voted second most luxurious hotel in England by TIME Magazine), Steinheuers (rated two Michelin stars) in Germany; and St. Louis Club in St. Louis, Missouri, a private and exclusive fine dining club.

Chef Hardel had the honor of serving as a guest chef for the president of Ecuador and many other important dignitaries throughout his career.

Menu

Amuse Bouche

❧ *Pot-Au-Feu of Foie Gras and Elephant Garlic Confit with Lee John's Organic Baby Vegetables*

❧ *Grilled Striped Sea Bass with Braised Baby Fennel and Caspian Sea Anchovies Escabeche*

❧ *Calvados Sorbet and Caramelized Fuji Apples*

❧ *Roasted Venison Loin with Winter Truffle Galette, Celery Root Mousseline, and Lavender Honey-Glazed Baby Brussel Sprouts*

❧ *Warm Pepper Goat Cheese of Chavignol Petite Mache Salad and Truffle Dressing*

❧ *Warm Bittersweet Chocolate Soufflé with Caramel and Vanilla Sauces*

Pot-Au-Feu of Foie Gras and Elephant Garlic Confit with Lee John's Organic Baby Vegetable

1 serving

1 duck bone

5 ounces foie gras

2 carrots

1 stalk celery

1 onion

2 cups white wine

1 stem of rosemary

1 stem of thyme

3 bay leaves

Salt and pepper

Elephant Garlic Confit
 (*see recipe that follows*)

Lee John's Organic Baby Vegetables
 (*see recipe that follows*)

Garnish: chervil; shaved foie gras

Roast the bone for 2½ hours at 325° to reach a golden color; then in stockpot sauté vegetables and add the bone, rosemary, thyme, and bay leaves. Add the white wine and cover. Cook slowly for about 5–6 hours. Strain the stock and add 3 ounces of foie gras and boil for 20 minutes; then take the foie gras out. Save remaining foie gras for the garnish.

Add all the cooked vegetables to the stock and warm on the stove. Before serving, add several slices of garlic confit and the remaining foie gras, shaved. Garnish with fresh chervil.

LEE JOHN'S ORGANIC BABY VEGETABLES

2 baby turnips

2 baby carrots

2 baby golden beets

4 pearl onions, red or yellow

1 stem celery

2 fingerling potatoes

Peel the vegetables and cook them in the duck stock.

ELEPHANT GARLIC CONFIT

1 elephant garlic

2 cloves garlic

1 stem thyme

1 stem rosemary

2 ounces duck fat

Salt and pepper

Put all ingredients into an ovenproof saucepan and bake at 175° for 3 hours.

Chef's Note
- It is better to cook vegetables separately to make sure you don't overcook one or the other.

© Vasyl Helevachuk. Shutterstock.

Grilled Striped Bass with Braised Baby Fennel and Caspienne Sea Anchovies Escabeche

1 serving

1 filet of striped bass

1 stem thyme

1 stem rosemary

Pinch of piment d'espelette

Sea salt

Extra virgin olive oil

Braised Baby Fennel
 (*see recipe that follows*)

Caspienne Sea Anchovies Escabeche
 (*see recipe that follows*)

Marinate the fish with the herbs and olive oil before grilling. To serve, put the baby fennel on the bottom of the plate, the striped bass on the fennel, and the escabeche around.

BRAISED BABY FENNEL

10 pieces baby fennel

1 tablespoon diced carrot

1 tablespoon diced celery

1 tablespoon diced onion

½ tablespoon diced garlic

1 tablespoon diced anchovies

¼ cup red wine

1 cup veal stock

1 stem of thyme

2 bay leaves

Salt and pepper

Clean the baby fennel and blanch it in boiling water for 1 minute; then submerge in ice and take the hairy part out.

Sauté the vegetables all together and add the baby fennel. Deglaze the pan with the red wine. Cook it down for 3–5 minutes; then add the veal stock and cook slowly for about 12 minutes.

CASPIENNE SEA ANCHOVIES ESCABECHE

10 pieces Caspienne Sea anchovies

½ ounce flat parsley

3 cups white wine vinegar

1 clove garlic

1 tablespoon cracked black pepper

2 juniper berries

½ lemon

½ onion

½ carrot

½ celery stem

¼ fennel

3 tablespoons sugar

7 fennel seeds

1 star anise

1/3 cup extra virgin olive oil

Finely dice (brunoise) all the vegetables; warm them with wine vinegar to 150°. Put the anchovies in a bowl and the vegetables and spices on the top; then put the warm white wine vinegar on the mix and add the olive oil.

© isidor stankov. Shutterstock.

Calvados Sorbet and Caramelized Fuji Apples

4 servings

1 teaspoon lemon juice

¼ cup sugar

¼ cup water

¼ cup corn syrup

2 tablespoons Calvados

2 Fuji apples

Boil the sugar, water, and corn syrup together and chill. Wash and core the Fuji apples and cut each into 8 slices. Combine the sugar syrup, Calvados, and lemon juice; juice the apples directly into the sugar syrup. Freeze in ice cream or sorbet machine.

CARAMELIZED FUJI APPLES

2 Fuji apples

2 tablespoons sugar

1 tablespoon butter

2 pinches cinnamon

¼ vanilla bean

Peel and chop the apples into ¼-inch dice. Caramelize the sugar and butter in a small sauté pan. Add the apples, scraped vanilla, and cinnamon. Sauté for 1 minute or until soft to the touch. Let cool at room temperature.

Roasted Venison Loin with Winter Truffle Galette, Celery Root Mousseline, and Lavender Honey-Glazed Baby Brussel Sprouts

1 serving

1 (6-ounce) venison loin steak

½ carrot

½ celery stem

½ onion

1 garlic clove

1 stem of thyme

1 bay leaf

1 cup of red wine

Winter Truffle Galette
    (*see recipe that follows*)

Celery Root Mousseline
    (*see recipe that follows*)

Lavender Honey-Glazed Baby Brussel
    Sprouts (*see recipe that follows*)

Marinate all the ingredients overnight; then take the venison out and put it on a paper napkin to absorb the extra red wine. Cook in a sauté pan.

Put the venison in the center of the plate, make a nice quenelle of the mousseline, put the brussel sprouts around and the galette on the venison.

CELERY ROOT MOUSSELINE

1 celery root, diced

3 shallots

2 cloves garlic

1 stem thyme

2 bay leaves

3 cups chicken stock

1 cup cream

In a stockpot, sauté the shallot and add the diced celery root; then add the garlic and the herbs and cook slowly for 3–5 minutes. Add the chicken stock; cook until the stock is evaporated and add the cream. Cook about 7 more minutes, slowly, and put in the blender to get a nice puree.

WINTER TRUFFLE GALETTE

2 sheets of phyllo dough

1 black winter truffle

1 onion

3 ounces apple-wood-smoked bacon

Salt and pepper

Cut the onion and bacon into a julienne size; then caramelize in a saucepan until it looks like a jam. Put the mixture in the refrigerator to cool.

Cut the phyllo dough in a round shape and bake for 10 minutes at 325°. Put the onion mix on the phyllo; then make a rosette of truffle on the top.

LAVENDER HONEY-GLAZED BABY BRUSSEL SPROUTS

3 ounces baby brussel sprouts

½ cup chicken stock

1 tablespoon lavender honey

Salt and pepper

Place the brussel sprouts into a saucepan with the lavender honey and the chicken stock. Cook slowly until liquid is gone and you start the process of glazing the brussel sprouts.

Warm Pepper Goat Cheese of Chavignol Petite Mache Salad and Truffle Dressing

1 serving

1 slice chavignol goat cheese

1 slice baguette bread

½ cup mache

2 cherry tomatoes

¼ teaspoon (approximately) cracked black pepper

Truffle Dressing (*see recipe that follows*)

Roll the cheese in the cracked black pepper to make like a crust and put it on the slice of baguette. Then bake it in the oven at 325° for 8–12 minutes.

Mix the mache and cherry tomato with the dressing. Put the salad on the plate and next to it the warm goat cheese.

TRUFFLE DRESSING

1 tablespoon truffle

1 tablespoon Xejes wine vinegar

3 tablespoons walnut oil

1 tablespoon Dijon mustard

Salt and black pepper

Put vinegar in a bowl and add salt, pepper, and mustard. Whip 1–2 minutes and add the walnut oil.

Warm Bittersweet Chocolate Soufflé with Caramel and Vanilla Sauces

5 servings

   7 ounces bittersweet chocolate

   3 tablespoons butter

   1 tablespoon cream

   4 egg yolks

   7 egg whites

   ½ teaspoon cream of tarter

   1/3 cup sugar

   Caramel Sauce (*see recipe that follows*)

   Vanilla Sauce (*see recipe that follows*)

Butter and sugar 5 (6-inch) ramekins. Set aside. Melt together the chocolate, butter, and cream. Whisk in the yolks and cool to room temperature. Whip the whites with the cream of tarter until foamy. Add the sugar and continue whipping until medium peaks are formed. Fold the egg white mixture into the chocolate mixture. Pipe or spoon the soufflé mixture into the ramekins, filling them to the top. Bake 350° for 18 minutes. Serve warm with sauces.

CARAMEL SAUCE

   1 cup sugar

   1 ounce butter

   1½ cups cream

   ½ vanilla bean

   2 pinches salt

In a stainless saucepan, combine sugar with ¼ cup water. Boil mixture and caramelize the sugar to a dark amber color. Slowly and carefully add the cream until combined. Add the butter, salt, and vanilla and lightly boil for 1 minute. Strain.

VANILLA SAUCE

   1 cup cream

   1 cup milk

   1/3 cup sugar

   4 egg yolks

   ½ vanilla bean, scraped

   Pinch salt

Bring the milk, cream, scraped vanilla bean, and sugar to a scald. Take off heat and cover for 20 minutes. Return to heat and bring to a boil. Whisk in one-fourth of the liquid with the egg yolks. Return egg yolk mixture to pot and whisk well. Strain and chill over ice bath.

The art of dining well is no slight art, the pleasure no slight pleasure.

—Michel de Montaigne

Practice Makes Perfect

Drink in the beauty, the drama, and the differences of both of my Mostly Mozart gala tables. This second of my favorite tabletops celebrating Mozart's musical genius is a contemporary table reminiscent of a fireworks display celebrating the genius's birthday.

Mozart's music washes away from the soul the dust of everyday life. In San Diego, California, the Mainly Mozart gala continues its yearly tradition of bringing together top players from major orchestras across the U.S., creating an all-star orchestra of virtuosos under the inspired leadership of Maestro David Atherton.

Nancy Laterno Bojanic, executive director of the organization, has been instrumental in taking this program into the schools, introducing over thirty-two thousand students in the U.S. and Mexico to the wonders of classical music.

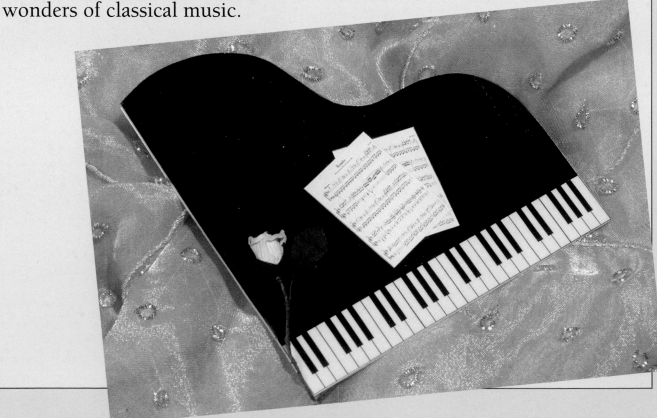

The Tabletop Landscape

The 250th anniversary of Mozart's birthday was a milestone that inspired me to celebrate with a fireworks display on my tabletop, and I found the ideal vase to start the celebration.

The four-foot contemporary vase was ringed with exploding red poppies and a second two-foot glass vase was placed between the poppies and filled with white Cala lilies jutting skyward, simulating an explosion of fireworks. Graceful vines drop to the table resembling the dying embers.

The tablecloth of sheet music (literally a king-size bedsheet) is edged with black and white fabric simulating piano keys. Black oversized napkins are held with silver square napkin rings engraved with the prodigy's name.

The silver matte greeting and menu card, embellished with a black piano and song notes, are wrapped with black and red ribbon.

Silver song notes hold black and silver place cards with a red miniature rose, following the color scheme, and silver silk organza bags hold a crystal votive candleholder for guests to take home.

Firelight flickers from candlesticks mimicking the Italian vase and surrounds the imposing centerpiece creating a magical glow, suggesting the falling lights from the firework display.

A contemporary tribute on this tabletop for a musical genius!

Quick Tips

- Black and white is always dramatic and can be used with any other accent color easily—black, white, and red; black, white, and yellow; or any other third color that you like.
- To embellish your menu card, find appropriate stickers at variety and stationery stores and stick on a corner, an easy way to continue your theme on the table.
- Follow the musical theme by printing your menu or your invitation on blank music sheets which you can buy at a music store.
- Use inexpensive musical instruments (found in children's stores) to tie on the back of every chair with musical-note-stamped ribbon. Fill trumpets and horns with silk flowers to match the color scheme.

ANDRÉ'S

Monte Carlo Resort and Casino
3774 South Las Vegas Boulevard
Las Vegas, Nevada

André Rochat

Executive Chef

André Rochat is Las Vegas' original celebrity chef and today, although he shares the limelight with some of America's most celebrated toques, chef Rochat remains the dean of Las Vegas chefs with three award-winning venues.

Since 1980, André's has been the most honored and respected restaurant in Las Vegas. It was recognized as the most popular restaurant in Las Vegas by the Zagat guide, received the prestigious DiRoNa award and has been honored with a 4 diamond triple AAA.

Since 1997, André opened the elegant chateau-style restaurant that bears his name at the Monte Carlo Resort and Casino, and in 2001 Alize at the top of the Palms Casino Resort which was recently selected by Condé Nast Traveler as one of the best 75 new restaurants in the world!

Menu

❧ *Crown of Artichoke Heart*

❧ *Crab Cakes*

❧ *Chicken Cream of Mushroom*

❧ *Phyllo-Wrapped Baked d'Anjou Pear and Roquefort Cheese on Baby Red Oak Salad with Roasted Walnuts and Pumpkin Seed Vinaigrette*

❧ *Traditional Dover Sole Veronique with Assorted Seasonal Baby Vegetables and Pommes Williams*

❧ *Jumbo Sea Scallops in Macadamia Nut Crust with Citrus Beurre Blanc*

❧ *Carmelized Atlantic Salmon, Sour Cream and Lime Sauce with Salmon Caviar and Potato Galette*

❧ *Chilean Sea Bass with Tangerine-Serrano Mojo*

❧ *André's Fresh Lemon Tart*

Crown of Artichoke Heart

8 servings

8 artichokes

Salt

Lemon juice

½ pound fresh goat cheese (1½ cups)

1½ cups heavy cream

Chopped fresh chives

1 tablespoon red wine vinegar

1 tablespoon olive oil

Freshly ground pepper

1 tomato, peeled and seeded (optional)

Garnish: goat cheese, chopped chives

Place artichokes in a large nonreactive pot and add cold water to cover. Add salt and bring to a boil. Cook until tender when pierced at the bottom with a knife tip, about 20 minutes.

Refresh under cold water; drain well. Remove leaves. Cut out fibrous choke in center of each heart. Trim sides of artichoke bottoms. Cut each heart into 8 equal pieces. Reserve on a plate; sprinkle with lemon juice to prevent discoloring.

In a large mixing bowl, crush fresh goat cheese with a fork. Slowly whisk in cream. Stir in chives, vinegar, and oil. Season with salt and pepper. Refrigerate for at least 1 hour.

Arrange sections of artichoke in the shape of a crown on 8 individual serving places. Interpose sections of peeled tomato, if desired. Garnish center of each place with a large spoonful of goat cheese and decorate with additional snipped chives, if desired.

Crab Cakes

4 servings

1 can Duugeness crab

Brunoise (small dice) of:

¼ pound red onions

¼ pound red bell pepper

¼ pound yellow bell pepper

4 tablespoons lemon juice

5 tablespoons mustard

2 teaspoons Worcestershire sauce

1 dash Tabasco

7 egg yolks (for egg wash)

1 cup breadcrumbs

salt and pepper

4 tablespoons butter

Garnish: 3 bunches chives

Begin with dry crabmeat (no juice at all). Add all ingredients at once except seasonings; add salt and pepper to taste. Make balls using a 6-ounce ice cream scoop; then flour the balls and dip in egg wash and then bread crumbs. Use a cookie cutter to shape crab cakes. In a large skillet, melt butter and sauté crab cakes over medium heat on each side over medium heat on each side until golden brown. Garnish with chives.

Chicken Cream of Mushroom

4 servings

4 large skinless chicken breasts

6 tablespoons bread flour

6 tablespoons butter

½ cup dry white wine

2 cups whipping cream

8 medium white mushrooms, sliced

Salt and pepper

Salt and pepper the chicken breasts and flour lightly. Over medium heat, melt the butter in a nonstick frying pan. Add the chicken breasts and brown on both sides. Add the sliced mushrooms and cook slowly.

When the mushrooms are cooked, add the wine and reduce to a syrup consistency. Add the cream and reduce, and add salt and pepper to taste

Phyllo-Wrapped Baked d'Anjou Pear and Roquefort Cheese on Baby Red Oak Salad with Roasted Walnuts and Pumpkin Seed Vinaigrette

4 servings

Extra fine phyllo dough
(12 x 17 inch sheets)

4 poached d'Anjou pears (canned in light syrup may be used)

¾ cup crumbled Roquefort cheese (or any creamy blue cheese)

¼ pound clarified butter (or melted butter)

1 ounce peanut oil

2 heads baby red oak greens, cleaned and washed*

Garnish: Candied Walnuts
(*see recipe that follows*),
1 large Roma tomato

Pumpkin Seed Vinaigrette
(*see recipe that follows*)

*Mesclun or any spring mix salad may be substituted.

Slice pears into strips and set aside to drain in a colander. Use a towel to blot pears dry. Place one sheet of phyllo on a smooth, dry surface. While working always keep the remaining phyllo completely covered with a damp towel and plastic wrap to avoid drying out. Using a pastry brush, apply melted butter to half the sheet. Fold sheet in half and turn 90 degrees. Once again brush half the sheet with butter and turn 90 degrees. Place pear slices (approximately ½ pear per wrap) in the middle of rectangle and top with 1 tablespoon of crumbled cheese. Fold top of dough over to cover the filling. Press with fingers to form a triangle around the filling. Cut off excess of dough, leaving enough to fold the edges to finish the triangle. Place the triangles in a pan coated with oil over medium heat and brown on all sides.

Cut the tomato in quarters; remove the seeds and cut in small even dices. Wash and trim the salad. Toss the baby red oak leaves with 1½–2 tablespoons dressing. Arrange in the center of the plate. Stand warm phyllo triangle in front of greens. Sprinkle with walnuts and tomato.

PUMPKIN SEED VINAIGRETTE

Yield: approximately 3 cups

1/3 cup oven-roasted pumpkin seeds

1 egg

1 teaspoon Dijon mustard

2 tablespoons sherry vinegar

1 cup pumpkin seed oil

Salt and pepper

In an electric blender, blend egg, mustard, sherry vinegar, and pumpkin seeds. Blend to puree. Slowly add pumpkin seed oil. (If mixture becomes too thick, you can add a little water.) Season with salt and pepper.

CANDIED WALNUTS

1 cup walnut halves

2 tablespoons clarified butter

2 tablespoons honey

Salt and pepper

¼ teaspoon cayenne pepper

Heat butter in pan on medium heat. Add walnuts, salt, pepper, and cayenne pepper. Stir to coat walnuts. Add honey; stir and remove from the heat. Continue to stir until walnuts are evenly coated. Set aside to cool.

Traditional Dover Sole Veronique with Assorted Seasonal Baby Vegetables and Pommes Williams

4 servings

4 whole Dover sole filets

6 tablespoons all-purpose flour

½ cup milk or half-and-half

Salt and pepper

½ cup clarified butter

Assorted seasonal baby vegetables (such as carrots, turnips, cauliflower fleuret)

2 teaspoons butter

Veronique Sauce (*see recipe that follows*)

Pommes Williams (*see recipe that follows*)

Garnish: chopped parsley

Preheat oven to 400°. Peel the skin off sole, starting from the tail. Cut off fins and head using a pair of scissors. Wash fish under running water. Place milk or half-and-half in a shallow dish and flour in another dish. Pass the sole first through the milk and then through the flour. Heat a large oven-proof frying pan with clarified butter and slowly fry the sole on one side until golden brown. Turn fish over and place entire pan in oven for 7–10 minutes. Remove from oven. Place fish on a baking sheet to rest for 5 minutes before removing the bones.

Lay the sole flat; pass a fish spoon down the middle of the fish, separating the filets. Carefully lift the filets from the top side of the fish and set aside; this will uncover the bones. Carefully lift the bones from the bottom filets, starting at the head side. The bones will lift off in one piece. The meat will stick to the bones if the fish is undercooked. Be sure to clean the fish of any small bones on the outside edges of the fish. Once all bones are removed, replace the top filets back on bottom filets to resemble the fish, which is now completely boneless.

Clean and blanch vegetables separately and glaze them in butter. Place the Dover sole on oval platter; place 5 grapes on top and spoon the sauce over. Sprinkle with chopped parsley. Arrange the vegetables and the potatoes around.

VERONIQUE SAUCE

2 sticks unsalted butter

Juice of 1 lemon

2 teaspoons demi-glace

20 green seedless grapes

Salt and pepper

Cook the butter on the stovetop until it gets a golden brown color; whisk in the lemon juice and demi-glace. Be careful when adding the juice, as the butter will foam and rise when liquid is added. Season to taste and add the washed green grapes to sauce, allowing the grapes to warm.

POMMES WILLIAMS

3 large Idaho potatoes

4 egg yolks

1½ ounces butter

Salt and pepper

Flour

Fine breadcrumbs

Frying oil

Garnish: 4 sprigs thyme

Quarter the potatoes and boil in salted water until soft. Strain the water and let the potatoes dry in a warm place for 10 minutes. Put through a ricer. Incorporate the yolks, butter, and salt and pepper. Do not overwork the mix. Break the mixture into fourths and shape into pears, using the flour to avoid sticking. Pass the potato shapes first in the egg wash, then in the breadcrumbs. At 275°, deep-fry until golden brown and cooked through the center. Garnish with sprigs of thyme.

Jumbo Sea Scallops in Macadamia Nut Crust with Citrus Beurre Blanc

4 servings

8 jumbo sea scallops

½ pound raw unsalted macadamia nuts

8 tablespoons flour

2 eggs

4 tablespoons unsalted butter

¼ cup cooking oil

Citrus Beurre Blanc (*see recipe that follows*)

Garnish: 4 sprigs of sweet basil, 4 pink
    grapefruit segments

Quickly rinse the scallops with cold water. Pat dry with a towel. Grate the macadamia nuts with a rotary cheese grater into a bowl. (Do not use a food processor; it turns the nuts into paste.)

Break the eggs and whisk them a little to make the egg wash. Salt and pepper the scallops; flour lightly. Pass the scallops through the egg wash and then through the grated nuts. Be sure the scallops are completely coated at each step. Refrigerate until ready to cook.

Preheat oven to 400°.

In an oven-proof frying pan over medium heat, add butter and oil. Brown scallops on one side; then turn carefully onto the other side. Place into preheated oven for approximately 3 minutes. The scallops should be golden brown and firm to the touch.

Place 1–1½ ounces beurre blanc on the bottom of the plate. Place 2 scallops in the center of the plate. Garnish with basil leaves and pink grapefruit segments.

CITRUS BEURRE BLANC

1 shallot, finely chopped

½ cup dry white wine

3 sticks unsalted butter, softened

Juice of 1 lime

Juice of 1 orange

Salt and pepper

In a pan, melt 1 ounce butter; add the shallots and sauté for 3 minutes; add the white wine and the citrus juice. Reduce to a syrup consistency. Emulsify the soft butter in the citrus juice with a whisk or hand blender. (Add the butter only little by little.) Season to taste. Keep warm. (Beurre blanc is served as a warm sauce. If it is too hot, it will break.)

Caramelized Atlantic Salmon, Sour Cream and Lime Sauce with Salmon Caviar, and Potato Galette

6 servings

- 6 (8-ounce) pieces of salmon fillet, skinned and deboned
- 3/4 cup sugar
- 1 teaspoon cayenne pepper
- 1½ teaspoons salt
- 6 sprigs of dill
- Sour Cream and Lime Sauce with Salmon Caviar (*see recipe that follows*)
- Potato Galette (*see recipe that follows*)

Mix all the seasoning ingredients in a bowl. Dip the top side of the salmon in the mixture. In a heavy-bottom frying pan, on high heat, put a small amount of vegetable oil, enough to coat the bottom of the pan. Place the salmon in it, the seasoned side down, and let it caramelize. Once caramelized, put the salmon, caramelized side up, on a greased small sheet pan and finish cooking it in a 380° degree oven for 5 minutes.

Place a warm potato galette in the center of each hot plate. Place the salmon on the top of the galette, caramelized side up. Add the salmon caviar to the sauce; mix in gently. With a spoon, pour some sauce around the salmon. Finish with a sprig of dill on the top of the salmon and serve.

POTATO GALETTE

- 2 medium White Rose potatoes
- 2 large eggs
- 1 tablespoon heavy cream
- ¾ cup butter
- 1 tablespoon minced chives
- 6 tablespoons all-purpose flour
- Salt and pepper

Put potatoes in a pot with enough cold water to cover them; add a little salt. Cook the potatoes thoroughly; then, while they are still hot, peel and mash potatoes with a food mill. With a whip, mix potatoes, eggs, flour, cream, chives, and salt and pepper. The mix should be soft but not liquid.

Melt butter in a heavy-bottom frying pan over medium heat. With a serving spoon, scoop the mix and place in frying pan to make a galette about 3 inches in diameter. You can also use a blinis frying pan, which would form the correct size of galette. Once each galette is brown on one side, turn it over and finish cooking slowly. Once cooked, keep warm until needed.

SOUR CREAM AND LIME SAUCE WITH SALMON CAVIAR

- 3/4 cup sour cream
- 2 tablespoons heavy cream
- 1 teaspoon salmon caviar
- Salt and fresh white pepper
- Juice and zest of 1 lime

In a small saucepan, heat the lime juice. Add the cream and sour cream. Season (do not over-salt, as the salmon caviar will add its share). Add the lime zest. Do not add the caviar until the very last minute, right before serving.

Chilean Sea Bass with Tangerine-Serrano Mojo

6 servings

6 (6-ounce) Chilean sea bass filets

2 tablespoons oil

Kosher salt and freshly ground black pepper

1 roasted red bell pepper, peeled, seeded, and sliced lengthwise ¼ inch thick

Tangerine-Serrano Mojo (*see recipe that follows*)

Garnish: tangerine segments (10–12 per plate)

Brush the fish with oil and season with salt and pepper. Cook the fish on a grill at medium heat. When ready to serve, spread the red bell pepper in the middle of the serving plate. Place the fish onto the peppers and ladle 1½ ounces mojo sauce over the fish. Garnish with tangerine segments.

TANGERINE-SERRANO MOJO

1 cup frozen concentrated orange juice

4–6 tangerines or 1 small can of tangerine sections in natural juice

2 serrano chilies, finely chopped

4 shallots, finely minced

2 tablespoons chives, finely chopped

¼ cup freshly squeezed lime juice

¼ cup lemon oil

1 tablespoon chopped parsley

1 tablespoon chopped cilantro

This sauce is to be served warm, not hot, so first just warm up the orange juice and add the tangerine segments, chilies, shallots, chives, lime juice, lemon oil, parsley, and cilantro, mix well and set aside.

To prepare tangerines for the sauce: Using a sharp paring knife, cut away the rind of the tangerines to expose the pulp; then cut between the segments alongside the thin membrane to remove the segments. Discard any seeds. If using canned tangerines, use segments only and discard the juice.

André's Fresh Lemon Tart

8 servings

1 cup flour

10 tablespoons butter, softened

6 tablespoons sugar

1 egg yolk

1 tablespoon heavy cream

Lemon Tart Filling (*see recipe that follows*)

Garnishes: lemon wedges; powdered sugar

Preheat over to 375°. Mix flour and sugar. Add soft butter, egg yolk, and cream until all ingredients are well incorporated. Do not overwork the dough. Let dough rest for approximately 20 minutes in a cool environment. Roll dough into a circle and place in a 9-inch tart pan, removing excess from rim. Puncture bottom of dough with a fork to avoid bubbling. Bake in preheated oven for 15–20 minutes, until golden brown. Remove from oven and cool. Pour filling into the tart shell and smooth the top with a spatula. Cool in refrigerator. Before serving, garnish with lemon slices; sprinkle with powdered sugar and brown with blow torch.

LEMON TART FILLING

6 whole eggs

5 egg yolks

1 cup fresh lemon juice

1½ cups sugar

Zest of 2 lemons

2 sticks butter, chopped into small pieces

In a stainless steel bowl, place whole eggs, yolks, lemon juice, lemon zest, and sugar. Place bowl in boiling bain-marie (or use a saucepan with water) and blend with a wire whip until the filling becomes a thick paste-like consistency. Remove from bain-marie and add butter; whip slowly.

Mozart Music washes away the dust of everyday life!

Chef's Note

- If you don't want to brown the top, you can pipe whipping cream instead.

Acknowledgments

To "Big Al My Pal," husband extraordinaire, without whose support, faith, and encouragement this book would not have been published.

To my children—Yvonne Rene, William Cory, and Michelle Marie—my fabulous Tuchscher kids, who have always been there for me through good times and bad.

To my extended family of children—Stephen Marks, Julie and Ron Rodgers, Michelle Hart, Arlene Pergamit, Steven and Nancy Krasnoff, Brad and Danielle Krasnoff—who always took an interest in my projects.

To my ten grandchildren—Matthew, Rachel, Mitchell, Colin, Chloe, Nathaniel, Cailen, Karlee, Mikila, and Spencer William—who fill my life with happiness, love to bake cookies with me, lick the frosting bowl clean, and always tell me I make the best cookies.

To my mother, who always had a beautiful table set when I got home from school and did it on a budget.

To Julia Cory Tuchscher, my mother-in-law, who completed my education in table setting and entertaining.

To Johanna Terry, my best friend, neighbor, right hand, left hand, and believer, who never let me down and was there for all the schlepping, and to her husband, Bill Terry, who loaned her to me countless hours day and night and didn't complain!

To my dear friend Barbara Cipranic, for always making me feel like I could do whatever I set out to do.

To my cousin Yolanda Brogger, an extraordinary interior designer, who always told me how proud she was of me and who brought all her friends to my seminars.

To Patsy Bentivegna, dearest friend, sister at heart, talented beyond belief, and an amazing chef whose recipes—especially dessert—are enough to make you believe that's why you are on earth.

To Bobbie Bohannon, who loves to entertain and set beautiful tables as much as I do, and who was always there when I yelled for help.

To Adrian Newell, manager of Warwick's Book Store in La Jolla, whose advice regarding this book was always appreciated and taken and who always took time out of her busy schedule to see me and review the progress of *Dining by Design*.

To Merridee Book, a talented publishing guru and very special friend whose advice was invaluable in making decisions regarding the design of the book. Thank you, Merridee!

To Tony Levas, owner of Levas & Son Draperies, for the beautiful tablecloths he made for all of the Mozart galas, and to Annette Stratton, his right hand, who saw to it that everything was completed on time.

To Ken and Penny Coley, owners of San Diego Flowers by Coley, and their creative staff, who were always in sync with what I visualized and executed to perfection each centerpiece I designed.

To Rosalynda Giannone and Maria Tostado, owners of Dreams Do Come True, for providing elegant specialty linens and chair covers whenever I needed them. Your selection and taste in linens is unsurpassed.

To Steve and Jan Shaw, owners of The Natural Touch and holiday designers for the Bellagio and Treasure Island, who took time away from their big projects to help me complete mine.

To Frank Lou from Bloomingdale's and our friend Donna Howard, who always helped me find the perfect china, stemware, silverware, and accessory pieces with patience, enthusiasm and a smile.

To Donna Vinton, Jan Toft, and Nancy Bliss from Don Janais, who never failed to ask how my book was coming and loaned me everything I asked for from their beautiful interior design showroom.

To Jonathan Jay and Grant Canfield for their patience and expertise in computers and PowerPoint and for coming to my aid every time I called. You will never know how much it meant!

To Lise Peyser, a friend who graces everything she touches with style, whose talent as an artist is unsurpassed and who always stood behind my ideas for tabletops.

To Jacqui Morris, who taught me everything I ever wanted to know about public speaking and took time to come and critique my seminars.

To Carolyn Clark, my beautiful and brilliant friend, who never failed to amaze me with her ideas, suggestions, and referrals and their phone numbers.

To Rochelle Rand, who called from New York and Paris when she found the latest and the greatest and made sure I knew where to find it.

To René Porter, incredible artist and creative soul, who helped me design and produce some of the wonderful invitations you see in this book.

To the management of Macy's Home Store in San Diego and Macy's Corporate in San Francisco, who invited me to do Dining by Design seminars at Macy's and never said "no" to anything I needed or wanted.

To Stacy Himmel, owner of India Ink Papers, for loving my invitation ideas, suggesting great changes and creating invitations for segments of this book.

Thank you Wendy Shames for the beautiful Dining Room you designed in La Jalla and extra hugs for letting me dress the table.

To George Hochfilzer and Eric Rimmele from the Westgate Hotel, for their enthusiasm and encouragement, being the first on board with fabulous recipes, and for providing access to Le Fontainebleau at their hotel to photograph the Mozart table shown in this book.

To George and Lise Peyser; Gayle McInnis; Mario and Kathy Matranga; Grant and Sandy Canfield; Barbara Cipranic; Steven Bernstein; and Admiral Leon "Bud" Edney and his lovely wife, Margon, who graciously opened up their homes to me for the photo shoots.

To Bloomingdale's, Neiman Marcus, Macy's Home Store, Bed Bath and Beyond, Pier 1, Tuesday Morning, Marshall's, Horchow Catalog, and Ikea for their wonderful array of merchandise and for their cooperation and good wishes, with a special thank-you to Palacek at the L.A. Mart® for the wonderful merchandise they sent me whenever I asked.

To the wonderful restaurants and chefs that so willingly participated in this project by creating menus and recipes for this book, with a special thank-you to Sally Graves from Commander's Palace, and Clay Bordan from American Properties.

To executive chefs Fabrice Hardel from Le Fontainebleau; George Hauer and Trey Foshee from George's at the Cove; André Rochat from André's Monte Carlo; Tory McPhail from Commander's Palace; Ken Irvine from K.R.I. Inc.; Patsy Bentivegna, private chef; Evan Cruz from Roy's La Jolla; Joe Busalacchi from Trattoria Fantastica; Mary Kay Waters and Andrew Spurgin from Waters Catering; Mineko Moreno, author of Sushi for Dummies; Steven Window and Sami Ladeki from Roppongis; Clay Bordan from Nectar, Santa Fe Salsa Company and Clay's La Jolla—thank you for completing my vision for a complete guide to entertaining.

Last but not least, to two of my favorite photographers—Roberto Zeballo and Larry Stanley—who are not only photographers but artists with passion, who captured the art of my tables through their lenses and their hearts. Thanks to each of you for helping me capture the true essence of my tables.

Thank you Saint Jude for answering my prayers regarding this book.

$1 of every book sold will go to St. Jude Research Hospital

Resources for Invitations

India Ink Papers

1907 Columbia Street
San Diego, CA 92101
(619) 234-4203
www.indiainkpapers.com

A retail store that specializes in custom invitations, with clients that include influential cultural and corporate groups. India Ink Papers is especially known for original wedding invitation designs.

Graphic designer Amy Kreft designed the invitations for "City Slickers Country Day" and "The Koi Pond."

René Porter Graphics

667 Fig Street
Chula Vista, CA
(619) 341-3389
RenePorter@sbcglobal.net

René Porter is a fine artist, illustrator, and graphic designer who trained at the Columbus College of Art and Design in Columbus, Ohio. Her skills allow her to take invitations from initial concept stage through completed, ready-to-mail invitations. René designed the invitations for "Living 'The Big Easy'" 'Birdhouse Couture," "The Art of the Table," "The Geisha and the Samurai," "Africa Adorned," "Style and Supper," "Tropical Nights in Paradise," and "Practice Makes Perfect."

Odd Balls

1004 Main Street
Pine Bluff, AR 71601
(870) 541-0173

"The best little paper company in Arkansas," established in 1991, Odd Balls provides the invitation and stationery industry with laser and inkjet compatible blank invitations featuring traditional, charming, mood-setting watercolor images to reflect the uniqueness of any event.

The product line includes invitations, response cards, place cards, fold-over correspondence notes, letter sheets, calling cards, and photo cards.

Odd Balls provided the invitations for "Seaside Soiree" and "The Prodigy and His Piano."

Picture Perfect

647 Hillcrest Industrial Boulevard
Macon, GA 31204
(800) 586-4144
www.picturep.com

Well known for its bright, whimsical look, Picture Perfect offers an important line that includes invitations, birth announcements, note cards, photo cards, calling cards, and scrapbooking items. Established in 1995, the company strives to push the envelope and develop new invitation ideas to excite the consumer and fill their clients' need to entertain with style.

Artist Susie Muise designed the invitation for "Willow Tree Garden Brunch."

DGInventive

1515 Central Avenue NE
Minneapolis, MN 55413
(800) 771-1574
www.dginventive.com

DGI began in 1949 and has grown to encompass three core businesses—print solutions, social stationery, and paper crafting products. The Paper Prince brand is the "designer boutique" of higher quality, affordably priced social expression products, providing consumers with the perfect invitation at an affordable price. DGI provided the invitation for "Autumn Harvest."

Resources for Floral Designs

San Diego Flowers by Coley

5075 Ruffin Road
San Diego, CA 92123
(858) 560-0464

With a passion for all things beautiful, Ken and Penny Coley of San Diego Flowers by Coley have spent the last forty-three years bringing beauty in the form of exquisite floral designs to weddings, private parties, and special events, including four presidential balls. As leaders in the floral industry, they provide florals for charity events as well as their clients' daily special occasions.

San Diego Flowers by Coley collaborated with author Olga Krasnoff to design the centerpieces for "Willow Tree Garden Brunch," "Birdhouse Couture," "The Art of the Table," "The Geisha and the Samurai," "Style and Supper," "The Prodigy and His Piano," and "Practice Makes Perfect."

Total Image

339 Crescent Bay Drive
Long Beach, CA 92651
(949) 500-0454

Owner Debby Neville has had an interest in design since importing antique pine furniture from England and Ireland in the late 1970s. After earning a degree in interior design from the Interior Designers Institute in Newport Beach, California, she practiced residential design in Orange County. She discovered a passion for flowers and studied floral design, a field that melded beautifully with interior design. Debby currently is a member of the faculty at the Interior Designers Institute, teaching both interior design and floral design. Debby took inspiration from Ron Dier's incredible ceramic shells to create a worthy centerpiece for "Seaside Soiree."

Alpine Mercantile

2101 Alpine Boulevard
Alpine, CA 01001
(619) 445-7090

Floral designer Kathy Matranga has always had a passion for flowers and loves to combine unusual flowers and different color combinations to create unique arrangements that are both fragrant and appealing.

Kathy has taught floral design at Grossmont College and has expanded her horizons as a floral designer for Alpine Mercantile where she is able to design creative arrangements for special events, weddings, and her favorite holidays—Christmas and Easter.

Since moving to the country, Kathy takes pride in the flowers she grows on the beautiful country estate she calls home. The buckboard floral arrangement for "City Slickers Country Day" was created by Kathy for the bruncheon she hosted for those city slicker friends she loves to entertain.

Tabletop Landscapes

987 Palencia Court
Chula Vista, CA 91910
(619) 216-1022
www.tabletoplandscapes.com

Using ordinary containers, unusual vessels, and personal collections of a variety of objects, author Olga Krasnoff creates spectacular centerpieces from casual to formal that create excitement and conversation at any event in which she participates. President of Tabletop Landscapes, Olga designed the centerpieces for "Living 'The Big Easy,'" "Tuscany Revisited," "Autumn Harvest," "The Koi Pond," "Africa Adorned," and "Tropical Nights in Paradise."

About the Photographers

Roberto Zeballos

(619) 656-2696
www.realestatebyphotos.com

San Diego photographer Roberto Zeballos has specialized in residential and commercial real estate architectural photography for twenty-one years and began his company to fulfill the need of the real estate community for excellence in photography. Roberto takes great pride in making each of his photographs a work of art.

Larry Stanley

(619) 723-0097
www.sd291.com

Photographer for Tiffany Silver Flatware 1845-1905 and former staff photographer for *Silver Magazine,* Larry Stanley also specializes in photographing commercial architecture, exterior construction, and residential interiors and photographs for master's degree students in architecture and interior design at San Diego State University.

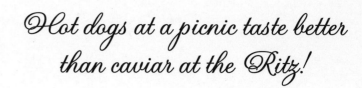

Hot dogs at a picnic taste better
than caviar at the Ritz!

It wouldn't be a picnic
without ants!

Celebrate

America the Beautiful

"Sit your guests down at a beautiful table and get up from your meal to a standing ovation!"

Olga K.

"Long after they forget the occasion they'll remember the setting."

Olga K.